GOD CALLS YOU
courageous

180
DEVOTIONS
AND PRAYERS
TO INSPIRE
YOUR SOUL

Carey Scott

GOD CALLS YOU
courageous

180
DEVOTIONS
AND PRAYERS
TO INSPIRE
YOUR SOUL

BARBOUR
PUBLISHING

Print ISBN 978-1-63609-115-0

Published by Barbour Publishing, Inc., 1810 Barbour Drive, Uhrichsville, Ohio 44683, www.barbourbooks.com

Our mission is to inspire the world with the life-changing message of the Bible.

WOMAN OF GOD,
YOU ARE
courageous!

What if you were able to overcome fear and insecurity to live a courageous life of faith? This kind of living is available to you, and it's made possible through a relationship with God. Let His Word create in you a bold and confident woman, one able to stand strong through the storms that come your way. The battles may make you weary and cause you to fear, but rest assured God sees them. He knows your struggles. And when you place your faith in Him and believe His promises to strengthen and save, the Lord will call you courageous.

STRENGTH TO FACE IT ALL

*I have the strength to face all conditions
by the power that Christ gives me.*
PHILIPPIANS 4:13 GNT

It's easy to feel weak and unable to weather the storms we face. Sometimes life comes barreling at us at warp speed and knocks us down. Sometimes everything that *can* go wrong *does*. And sometimes it seems we're being bombarded on every side. It's in those moments we want to wave the white flag in defeat, lick our wounds, and retreat to safer places.

But that's not what God wants for you. His hope is that you'll remember Jesus' promise to strengthen you for anything and everything and invite Him into the mess. Friend, you're not alone in the battles. When your faith is securely anchored in Him, nothing is impossible. Nothing in life is too formidable. No situation has to be too overwhelming and no person too overpowering. With the Lord's help, you can face it all fearlessly. And when you do, God will call you courageous!

God, there are times it all feels too much, and I feel the weakness of being human. My anxiety skyrockets as my heart starts to beat out of my chest. All I think about is running away and hiding from the things that feel threatening. Fill me with the power of Christ so I can stand courageous as I trust You. In Jesus' name I pray. Amen.

NEVER ALONE

"Be strong and courageous. Don't tremble! Don't be afraid of them! The LORD your God is the one who is going with you. He won't abandon you or leave you."
DEUTERONOMY 31:6 GW

What scares you the most? What's happening in your life that causes anxious thoughts? Where is your worry coming from right now? The truth is there are countless situations that can make us tremble with fear. Often they trigger memories from other times we've felt similarly. And a common thread through them all is feeling like we're all alone, left to figure things out by ourselves. So not only are we terrified of what's ahead, but we're depressed about being an island.

But take heart, friend! While the fear may be real and something to conquer, you have the Lord your God with you. Scripture tells us that He will never leave you. He will never forsake you. And even more, He is right there—right now—with you. So when you feel the heat of hopelessness, be quick to cry out and ask to feel His presence in your situation. That act of courage doesn't go unnoticed by the Lord. To the contrary, it delights Him, and He will act.

God, I'm drowning in fear and unable to function.
Please come quickly and bring peace to my life and courage
to my heart. I need You! In Jesus' name I pray. Amen.

HE'LL HOLD YOU STEADY

*"Don't panic. I'm with you. There's no need to fear
for I'm your God. I'll give you strength. I'll help you.
I'll hold you steady, keep a firm grip on you."*
<small>ISAIAH 41:10 MSG</small>

Sometimes it's frustrating when people tell you not to be concerned. They aren't the ones in your situation. They aren't the ones having to manage the fear you're feeling. They won't have to walk out the consequences if your greatest worries come to pass. And rather than be a support, they pile heaps of discouragement on your shoulders. Often our earthly support just doesn't know how to hold us up when we're underwater.

What a relief to know God not only understands the very minute details of what we're battling, but is actively guiding us through it. Victory with Him is guaranteed. And every time your knees feel weak and your heart feels overwhelmed, ask God to hold you up. He will give you strength to take the next step. He will give you confidence to stand strong. And even more, He will call you brave for asking for help.

*God, hold me tight. Don't let me go. I need You to keep
me steady as I wade through the things that scare me.
Strengthen me by Your hand and help me trust that
You have my back. In Jesus' name I pray. Amen.*

GOD ABOVE OTHERS

But those who trust in the LORD for help will
find their strength renewed. They will rise on
wings like eagles; they will run and not get
weary; they will walk and not grow weak.
ISAIAH 40:31 GNT

Trusting God to help us when we're anxious is crucial. While our friends and family may have the best intentions, they don't trump the Lord's abilities. They might have hard-won wisdom to share, but God's wisdom is far above. They may sacrifice time and treasure to join us on the battlefield because they love us deeply, but God's love is perfect. So our best bet is to grab onto the Lord the moment the fear begins to creep in and hold on for dear life.

Where do you need renewed strength today? Are you struggling in marriage, weary from the fight? Are you battling your teenager, trying to parent them to better choices? Maybe your health is failing, and wholeness feels hopeless. Are your finances a mess and the money that needs to go out doesn't match the money coming in? Maybe you're about to step out of your comfort zone and try something new, and you're scared. When you ask Him, God will give you strength for it all. And the courage you show in asking delights His heart.

God, please give me strength for what I'm facing.
Let me press into You to meet every need,
every time. In Jesus' name I pray. Amen.

YOUR HOPE AND HELP

And that about wraps it up. God is strong, and he wants you strong. So take everything the Master has set out for you, well-made weapons of the best materials. And put them to use so you will be able to stand up to everything the Devil throws your way.
EPHESIANS 6:10–12 MSG

Today's verse reminds us that God will give us everything we need to stand strong. No matter what it is—courage, confidence, wisdom, peace, discernment, joy, hope—the Lord promises it to you in spades. Whatever you need from Him to get through the struggles that barge into your life, it is yours for the taking. God never intended for you to walk through this life alone. His plan wasn't for you to be your own savior. His creation of community wasn't so others would have all the answers you need. From the beginning, God's design has been for Him to be your hope and help no matter what.

Be confident in this truth, sweet one. Latch onto the powerful promises from today's verse. Don't wait any longer. Spend time in prayer today asking for what you need. All of God's resources are available to those He loves. . .and that means you! God savors your courage. Go ahead and use it.

God, thank You for knowing my needs even before I do. Thank You for being willing to give me all I need to navigate fear and insecurity. In Jesus' name I pray. Amen.

YOU HAVE A DEFENDER

"The LORD is my strong defender; he is the one who
has saved me. He is my God, and I will praise him,
my father's God, and I will sing about his greatness."
EXODUS 15:2 GNT

In those moments when you feel no one is on your side, don't become discouraged. Don't think this is the best it will get and give in to hopelessness. Sometimes we choose to throw in the towel because the heat is too hot. We let despair be the banner we wave. And rather than trust God as our defender, we decide the fight isn't worth the energy and emotion. We decide as long as we get relief from the pressure, fear gets to win. Where is our faith?

Listen up, warrior. You may feel tired and weary. You may be ready for this long season of hardship to be over. Your heart may be grieved by a lack of meaningful community. It may seem like things will never be good again. But God has been your Defender from the beginning. He has been there fighting for you. Ask for the eyes to see His hand, and let it be what gives you confidence to take the next step with intentionality, knowing He calls you courageous.

God, thank You for being my Defender, even when
I didn't realize it. I praise Your holy name and recognize
Your greatness! In Jesus' name I pray. Amen.

THE COURAGE TO SAY NO

There isn't any temptation that you have experienced which is unusual for humans. God, who faithfully keeps his promises, will not allow you to be tempted beyond your power to resist. But when you are tempted, he will also give you the ability to endure the temptation as your way of escape.

1 CORINTHIANS 10:13 GW

With His help, you can say no. If you let it, your willpower can be fueled supernaturally by the Holy Spirit, giving you the ability to resist any temptation that comes your way. Be it a piece of chocolate cake, a flirtatious moment with a coworker, an overpriced purse, a cheat sheet, a little white lie, or something else that goes against your resolve, you can resist with His help. Even more, God knows your limits, and He promises not to push you past them. So that means you will always be able to find divine courage to refuse.

Remember, when you invite the Lord into those moments of temptation and ask for His strength, it will be given to you. He knows it takes courage to do the right thing over what your flesh wants. He knows the grit involved in setting and keeping personal boundaries. And, friend, He calls you brave!

God, help me stand strong and be resolved to do the right things. Keep my eyes focused on Your promise to save me. In Jesus' name I pray. Amen.

MEDITATE ON THE MIRACLES

"Sing to him. Make music to praise him. Meditate on all the miracles he has done. Brag about his holy name. Let the hearts of those who seek the LORD rejoice. Search for the LORD and his strength. Always seek his presence."
1 CHRONICLES 16:9–11 GW

It's so important for us to remember the ways God has helped us in the past. When you feel weak, think back to a moment when the Lord infused you with courage. Think about when that surge of confidence pushed you out of your comfort zone and into something new. What about when you bravely stood up for yourself, an out-of-character move that caught you off guard? Can you remember a time when you took that fearless leap of faith and it paid off? What about when you were gutsy enough to make the first move, or to boldly refuse to go along with the crowd? God is so pleased by your faith. He sees every decision and calls you courageous!

So hold on to these intrepid moments, giving thanks to God for filling you with the ability to overcome fear and insecurity to do what was right. And let these memories be what fuels you to be brave the next time.

God, what an honor to meditate on all the miracles of courage You've given me over the years. Thank You! In Jesus' name I pray. Amen.

MODELING BRAVERY

That precious memory triggers another: your honest faith—and what a rich faith it is, handed down from your grandmother Lois to your mother Eunice, and now to you! And the special gift of ministry you received when I laid hands on you and prayed—keep that ablaze!

2 TIMOTHY 1:5-6 MSG

One of the most compelling reasons we must overcome fear and learn to live bravely is that we're being watched. How we walk out our life matters to others. If we model anxiety, we inadvertently teach others to live with it. If we worry all the time, chances are others will follow suit. If we allow fear to inform every decision we make, we're effectively training the next generation to do the same. We just can't be okay with this.

What if instead we leaned into Jesus Christ, trusting Him to lead us? What if we chose faith over fear? His promise to be our Protector never expires. He never wavers in His love for us. And when we understand what's at stake if we pass fear down to others, God may be our only hope to live differently. When you put your trust in the Lord, you delight His heart. He sees your decisions to model boldness, and He will call you courageous.

Dear God, teach me to be brave so I can be an example to others. Help me live with confidence and courage. In Jesus' name I pray. Amen.

YOU WEREN'T CREATED TO BE TIMID

*For the Spirit that God has given us does not make us timid;
instead, his Spirit fills us with power, love, and self-control.*
2 TIMOTHY 1:7 GNT

When God created you, He didn't make you to be fearful. You weren't designed to be cowardly or apprehensive. He didn't intend for you to choose panic over peace or trepidation over tranquility. Instead, His Spirit empowers you with amazing attributes—things like power, love, and self-control. All these decidedly trump any fear that may creep into your heart.

Keep this truth in mind, because it's a game changer. In those times when your courage is waning, remember that fear isn't from God. And once you recognize it, ask the Lord to fill you with confidence. Ask for grit. Ask Him to clear your head of lies and replace them with truth. Tell Him exactly what you need to withstand the situation at hand, or if you don't know, simply ask for His help. Pressing into your faith shows courage, and it delights Him!

*Dear God, sometimes feeling courageous seems impossible.
There are too many things that scare me. There are situations
where I feel intimidated and unable to conquer. I need to
remember the Holy Spirit's promise to fill me with all I need to
be brave and to stand in that truth. In Jesus' name I pray. Amen.*

IT'S A COMMAND

"I have commanded you, 'Be strong and courageous!
Don't tremble or be terrified, because the LORD
your God is with you wherever you go.' "
JOSHUA 1:9 GW

God actually commands us to be brave. He isn't merely suggesting we put on our big-girl pants. He isn't holding His divine breath that we'll wear a brave face as we waddle through a difficult time. His fingers aren't crossed in hopes that some semblance of courage comes together as we move forward. Friend, God is commanding you to be strong and brave.

Why does He expect this of us? How does the Lord think we can pull this off? It's because He promises to go with us. He won't leave you alone, waiting to see if you'll muster the grit to stand tall. No. The entire force of heaven will be closer than your breath. So when you're terrified to speak up or make the next move or when you're feeling insecure and unable to take meaningful action, remember He is right there with you. Be bold enough to step out in faith, and He will call you courageous.

> *God, thank You for commanding courage. It takes*
> *so much faith, so please increase mine so I can*
> *follow Your directive. Help me trust You even*
> *when I feel terrified. In Jesus' name I pray. Amen.*

COURAGE TO ADMIT WEAKNESS

But his answer was: "My grace is all you need, for my power is greatest when you are weak." I am most happy, then, to be proud of my weaknesses, in order to feel the protection of Christ's power over me. I am content with weaknesses, insults, hardships, persecutions, and difficulties for Christ's sake. For when I am weak, then I am strong.

2 CORINTHIANS 12:9–10 GNT

So often the idea of embracing our weaknesses, let alone feeling proud of them, goes against everything we know. We boast about our accomplishments and the times we prevailed through adversity, but rarely do we choose to highlight the times we felt inadequate or pathetic. It seems ridiculous to be proud of those occasions. But God's ways are not our ways, and His thoughts are not our thoughts. And without a doubt, the Lord's ways are best.

So when He says our weakness opens the door for His strength, it makes sense that our feebleness is worth celebrating. With that perspective, we can even be content with our weakness because we know God will make up the difference in glorious ways! He will fill in the gaps with His goodness! Yes, it takes courage to admit you're weak. But when you do, God smiles with approval.

God, I confess my weaknesses in great expectation of Your power showcased in my life! In Jesus' name I pray. Amen.

BOLD LIVING

Keep your eyes open, hold tight to your convictions, give it all you've got, be resolute, and love without stopping.
1 CORINTHIANS 16:13–14 MSG

In all you do, be determined. Be unwavering in your faith as you trust God through the unknown. Be alert, keeping your eyes open and watchful. Know what you believe and hold it tightly. And love without ceasing, even when it's hard. This is how God wants you to live out your days on earth. Honestly, it can be a scary way to live, because our humanity sets us up to fail—and who doesn't have a fear of failing?

This is where our faith comes into play. This is why we need to trust the Lord with all our heart rather than lean on our own understanding. Our ability to live with this kind of intentionality comes from the Lord. His expectation isn't for you to be perfect but rather purposeful. And because it takes courage to live this way, know that God recognizes your boldness and applauds it.

God, trying to live the way You desire is intimidating because I'm afraid of failing and letting You down. Would You boost my confidence in everything I do through You? Help me remember that Your heart for me is good and I can do all things with Your help. In Jesus' name I pray. Amen.

DON'T EVER FORGET

"In a few minutes you're going to do battle with your enemies. Don't waver in resolve. Don't fear. Don't hesitate. Don't panic. GOD, your God, is right there with you, fighting with you against your enemies, fighting to win."
DEUTERONOMY 20:3–4 MSG

When we stare at what scares us, it's easy to feel weak and unable to weather the storm. Somehow the things we fear seem formidable and we can't help but cower under them. We decide we're the weak one and give up. Rather than stand in strength, we panic and retreat. We buckle under the pressure to be brave. When we find these words and descriptions to be true, chances are it's because we've forgotten one very important truth: We are not alone.

How would your mindset change if you really believed God was right there with you? What would happen to your courage if you realized He was in the fight alongside you? Does knowing that He is always victorious increase your confidence? One of the greatest gifts we're given is the presence of God. It's a game changer. And when you fully embrace all the ramifications of His presence, you will be an overcomer. Even more, God will call you courageous.

God, what an honor to know that You love me enough to be with me always. Be it in peace or in battle, I know I can count on Your presence to support me. Thank You! In Jesus' name I pray. Amen.

HE NEVER GROWS WEARY

Don't you know? Haven't you heard?
The eternal God, the LORD, the Creator of the
ends of the earth, doesn't grow tired or become
weary. His understanding is beyond reach.
ISAIAH 40:28–29 GW

Thankfully, God never tires. He never becomes too weary for the battle. But we do. Think back to a time when you just gave up. All the details became too much to manage and you felt as if you had no choice but to walk away. Maybe you felt hopeless. Maybe the road ahead looked too slippery, and turning around felt like the only smart choice. Take a moment to thank the Lord that He never gives up on us or the scary situations we find ourselves in.

The next time life feels too big, ask the Lord for bold confidence to live unshaken. Ask Him to show you the path He has planned for your life. Trust God to infuse you with strength and wisdom to know what's right. Let Him bring clarity to end any confusion. And the Lord will call your faith courageous and beautiful.

God, I'm so glad You never grow weary or tired, because
that means You'll always be available when I do. Thank
You for the endless supply of strength and courage
when I need them most. In Jesus' name I pray. Amen.

THE POWERFUL WORD OF GOD

Whatever was written beforehand is meant to instruct us in how to live. The Scriptures impart to us encouragement and inspiration so that we can live in hope and endure all things.

ROMANS 15:4 TPT

When you're feeling inadequate for the job or defenseless in the argument, look to the Word of God for encouragement. In those times when your heart feels unprotected and your self-worth vulnerable, grab your Bible immediately. When you're spineless to act or timid to speak up, let His Word inspire you to make a move in the right direction. The simple truth is you cannot live well if you're not digging into scripture. It offers answers to everything you'll ever face, giving hope as well as the strength to endure whatever comes your way.

So be full of confidence because the Lord hasn't hung you out to dry. He isn't hoping you'll figure things out on your own. God isn't hiding the answers, hoping you'll be able to find them. Instead, He lovingly filled His Holy Word with wisdom and discernment for you. And He's hoping you'll have the courage to open it up.

God, sometimes I get confused by all the details and end up scared as I try to navigate this life well. I need encouragement and direction, so thank You for giving me Your Word. I will cherish it! In Jesus' name I pray. Amen.

HOW TO RENEW YOUR STRENGTH

*But those who trust in the Eternal One will
regain their strength. They will soar on wings as
eagles. They will run—never winded, never weary.
They will walk—never tired, never faint.*
ISAIAH 40:31 VOICE

So often we lack the kind of endurance our life requires. We get tired of the day in and day out details that ask so much of us because we just want things to be okay and go back to normal. We want to curl up on the couch with a cup of coffee and a good book and let the rest of the world disappear. Sometimes adulting gets to be overwhelming. So much is at stake, and it scares us.

The Bible says that if we choose to trust God, the benefit is a renewal of strength. How does that work? When we release control—the control created by fear—we're asking the Lord to take over. And that act of surrender allows Him to fuel us with His power to keep going. Yes, letting go of the wheel can be scary. It takes a hearty dose of faith. But when you do, God will call you—His beloved—courageous.

*God, I surrender my will to Yours. I surrender my plans to
Yours. I am choosing to trust You to guide my life and give
me the strength to walk it out. In Jesus' name I pray. Amen.*

HE DOESN'T WORK THAT WAY

"God is my savior; I will trust him and not be afraid.
The LORD gives me power and strength; he is my savior."
ISAIAH 12:2 GNT

We're told not to be afraid repeatedly in the Bible, but what if we are afraid? We may have the best intentions to put our faith over fear, but what if we can't? What if we continue to come up short? Not only are we suffering, but now we also feel like a bad Christian. We're sure the Lord is mad at us since we can't seem to figure out how to trust. The voice in our head continues to whisper, *You've done it this time*. And because our feelings of insecurity are screaming, we are too afraid to ask for His help, certain the answer is no.

Friend, God doesn't work that way. He doesn't judge you, because the blood of Jesus took care of His wrath. Now He sees you through the lens of compassion and love, having mercy for the things that bog you down. Be it worry, weakness, or weariness, God wants to hear it all. And He promises to meet your every need. Be fearless and ask Him for help. He sees that kind of courage as noteworthy.

God, help my unbelief so I can trust in You
for all things. In Jesus' name I pray. Amen.

GUARDED BY GOD HIMSELF

*He will keep you from every form of evil or calamity
as he continuously watches over you. You will be
guarded by God himself. You will be safe when you
leave your home, and safely you will return. He will
protect you now, and he'll protect you forevermore!*

Psalm 121:7–8 tpt

You can breathe deep because you're guarded by God Himself. Think about that for a moment. The One who spoke the heavens and earth into being, who created every living creature, stands guard over you every moment of every day. He is actively protecting you this very second. And this level of defense won't ever stop. Friend, let go of the fear that's eating you up. You can exhale.

It may feel hard to trust in Someone you can't see, but faith requires it. You choose to believe. And chances are you've seen His fingerprints all over your life. You've experienced healing or restoration. You've seen provision and deliverance. You've felt the peace that surpasses all understanding. Let these times give you the courage to trust Him again, knowing He stands guard over your life. And hear Him call you brave.

*God, what a powerful reality. I never knew You guarded
me Yourself. I'm humbled and grateful. Make me
confident in that truth! In Jesus' name I pray. Amen.*

COURAGE TO TRUST

Lord, so many times I fail; I fall into disgrace. But when I trust in you, I have a strong and glorious presence protecting and anointing me. Forever you're all I need!
PSALM 73:26 TPT

Too often we rely on ourselves for protection. We put up barriers and walls in hopes of keeping our heart safe. We insulate with elaborate defenses that effectively close us off from meaningful community. And because we are too afraid to trust anyone but ourselves, we live a small life full of over-the-top caution. How would things be different if we chose to trust God instead? What if we decided to embrace His glorious presence as our protection?

Talk to the Lord today about all the times you were unable to save yourself. Share about painful moments when others let you down. Unpack why trusting Him stirs up fear in your heart, and ask for a renewed spirit of hope. Ask for courage to trust Him above all, and then take that step of faith. Not only will it help to heal your heart, but God will see it and call you courageous!

God, I'm not good at trusting. Too many times it has backfired. But I can't navigate this life on my own, so I'm putting myself out there again. Please build my confidence in You as I place my faith in You. In Jesus' name I pray. Amen.

THE REWARD OF WAITING

Let your hope keep you joyful, be patient
in your troubles, and pray at all times.
ROMANS 12:12 GNT

Whoever said patience is a virtue needs a talking-to. Amen? For most of us, waiting isn't our strong suit. We've been conditioned to want things right away. Immediate gratification, if you will. We look for the express lane to everything in life, getting frustrated if we must wait for anything. So when life slaps us upside the head, we crave an instant fix. When we find ourselves fearful, we expect the remedy to present itself right away. When our insecurities are screaming, we frantically look for a quick way to silence them. It's learned behavior.

But God rewards patience. He knows waiting requires faith, and that posture pleases Him. Anytime you choose to trust in the Lord over yourself, He is delighted. Every time you take a deep breath rather than react with worry, He smiles. When you decide to believe the Lord's truths instead of adopting an anxious heart, He is thrilled to no end. And when you are weighed down by fear but choose to wait for God to act, He calls you courageous.

God, I confess that I don't like waiting. Life moves fast,
so it goes against what feels normal. Help me learn
patience, because I know it not only pleases You but
greatly benefits me. In Jesus' name I pray. Amen.

FEARING NO ONE

*The LORD is my light and my salvation;
I will fear no one. The LORD protects me
from all danger; I will never be afraid.*
PSALM 27:1 GNT

Fear is a big deal, and sometimes we feel it because of those around us. Think about it for a moment. What role does fear play in your life? Are there people who scare you for one reason or another? Are you afraid of their opinions, or maybe the wrath of their judgment? Are you scared of being rejected or abandoned? Do you feel controlled or manipulated? Maybe you live with people who are emotionally unsafe and hurt your feelings regularly. In these instances, just being around them stirs up fear.

When you put your faith in the Lord, your confidence will grow as you trust His truths in your life. Knowing who God is and who He created you to be will strengthen your sense of value. You won't spend time worrying about what others may think because you'll believe that what God thinks matters more. In the end, there won't be anyone left to fear. And God will call that kind of personal resolve courageous.

*God, too often I've let the fear of others be a driving
force in my life. Rather than stand in the truth of who
I am because of You, I've cowered. Help me be brave
enough to trust You. In Jesus' name I pray. Amen.*

YOUR FEARLESSNESS COMES FROM HIM

Counting on GOD's Rule to prevail, I take heart and gain strength. I run like a deer. I feel like I'm king of the mountain!
<small>HABAKKUK 3:19 MSG</small>

Feeling like a conqueror is a spectacular sensation. When we've faced down those things that have caused us fear and are still standing strong, we feel a sense of triumph. We know we are overcomers. And we recognize that we survived what could have taken us out. To have a faith that is firm enough to prevail over fear is an awesome feeling. In times of triumph, do you give the glory to God?

The truth is that we're strong women. We are capable in so many important ways. And we all have a measure of courage for dealing with the hard situations life brings our way. But, friend, it's important to recognize the Lord's hand in them all. We gain strength through Him. We find our footing with His help. We are brave in His power. We have mountaintop moments because of His goodness. Make sure to thank Him for seeing your need for courage and confidence and giving them to you in His perfect timing.

God, today I want to thank You for being my biggest cheerleader. You are why I can live and love with purpose and passion. You are why I can be fearless. I love You! In Jesus' name I pray. Amen.

YOUR PART TO PLAY

Be brave. Be strong. Don't give up.
Expect GOD to get here soon.
PSALM 31:24 MSG

What a powerful call to those who battle with fear. This verse offers a great reminder that we have a part to play in the victory over anxiety. Too often we roll over in defeat. We sit and sulk, hoping something changes soon. We complain to anyone who will listen. We amplify our anxiety through our words and actions. And we buckle under the weight of worry. Let's do things differently.

The psalmist is asking you to stand in your faith. Even when everything around you looks scary and hopeless, with His help it's not. God is the key to your ability to take that next step with confidence. So press into the Lord so you can be brave in these kinds of situations. Let Him encourage you that things will work out, and stay engaged. Place your hope and expectation in His promise to save. Do these things and listen as God calls your choices courageous!

God, I confess the times I've given up. Forgive me
for being lazy and inactive in my own life. I have
been ineffective too often. Starting today, I'm changing.
I'm going to take an active role—with Your help—in standing
up and engaging. I'm going to draw my strength and
courage from You and be brave. In Jesus' name I pray. Amen.

ON THE CLIFF-EDGE OF DOOM

*God is a safe place to hide, ready to help when we
need him. We stand fearless at the cliff-edge of doom,
courageous in seastorm and earthquake, before the rush
and roar of oceans, the tremors that shift mountains.*
PSALM 46:1–2 MSG

- -

Think back to a time when you were on the cliff-edge of doom. Maybe
it was a season when your marriage was on the brink of divorce. Maybe
your child had serious medical issues and doctors couldn't get them
under control. Maybe your career was derailed by a jealous coworker
and now you're unemployed. It's times like these when we feel hopeless,
helpless, and terrified things won't work out in the end.

If you'll let Him, God will meet you at the cliff's edge. He'll be there
with open arms and encouragement, ready to scoop you up. His presence is always just what you need when life seems to be falling apart.
He will melt your fears away, calm the storm raging in your heart. And
when you surrender yourself into His care, the Lord will call you His
courageous one.

*God, I'm at the edge of the cliff right now and
desperate for Your help. I'm scared and sad
and ready for a break. Please help me be brave
as I navigate this difficult situation. I can't do
it without You. In Jesus' name I pray. Amen.*

WHEN YOU NEED IT AGAIN

And now, GOD, do it again—bring rains to our drought-stricken lives so those who planted their crops in despair will shout "Yes!" at the harvest, so those who went off with heavy hearts will come home laughing, with armloads of blessing.
PSALM 126:4–6 MSG

Sometimes we worry that since God has already rescued us once, He won't do it again. We're afraid we've used our one and only get-out-of-jail-free card and now we're on our own. We mistakenly believe that He's probably frustrated we're somehow back in a mess again. And so rather than ask God to help, we silently suffer. If that's you, let today's verse encourage your spirit!

The psalmist shows us that we can ask over and over for His intervention. As a matter of fact, God wants us to! Don't be afraid to go to the Lord every time there's a kink in the road. His plan from the beginning has been to be your shelter and strong tower. He wants to be the One who meets your every need. And He will bring provision and blessing. Be the kind of woman who boldly takes God up on His promise to do it again. It's that kind of faith He calls courageous.

God, give me the confidence to ask You over and over again for help. Don't let me sit in despair and hopelessness. Instead, let me have bold faith in Your promises! In Jesus' name I pray. Amen.

THE COURAGE TO LOVE BIG

"You are to love the Lord Yahweh, your God, with a passionate heart, from the depths of your soul, with your every thought, and with all your strength. This is the great and supreme commandment."

MARK 12:30 TPT

Putting it all out there can be scary. It's not that we don't want to love big, but we remember the times it backfired on us. We think about how our feelings got hurt when our love for someone wasn't returned, or how others used our commitment to them as a way to manipulate us. We are frankly terrified at the idea of loving so completely, and so we love in part. We keep up walls as protection. And we patrol them with fervor.

So when we read a scripture that tells us to go all in with loving the Lord, we might want to put on the brakes instead. He wants us to love Him with passion from the depths of our soul, with every thought and all our strength. For those who have been burned, this prospect is terrifying. But, friend, God can be trusted. It may be a leap of faith for you, but that brave choice will prompt the Lord to call you courageous!

God, heal my heart so I can love You big. I need a bigger measure of faith, and I know You will give it to me. In Jesus' name I pray. Amen.

SCARED TO STOP

"Come to me, all who are tired from carrying heavy loads, and I will give you rest."
MATTHEW 11:28 GW

Sometimes in our fear and worry, we work tirelessly to fix things. We try to find ways to improve our health, heal a heart, repair a relationship, pay a bill, forgive an offense, or finish the work. We're afraid that if we stop moving forward at full speed, everything will end in disaster. In our anxiety, we carry the burden alone because we struggle to trust anyone else with it. And when we lay our head on the pillow at night, we realize we're exhausted. We feel every bit of our human limitations. And often even our sleep is robbed because we can't seem to shut off our minds. We're scared to stop worrying.

Friend, it takes real courage to ask for help. Being vulnerable is scary. But being a woman of faith means you choose to believe God anyway. He never sleeps or stops, which means you can. The Lord will never give up on you and what weighs heavily on your heart. You can trust a known God with an unknown future because He is fully able and completely willing to help you. Let Him see your courage!

God, You know my heart and all that weighs on it.
I surrender my fears and insecurities to You. I'm choosing
to let You take it from here. In Jesus' name I pray. Amen.

UNSHAKABLE AND ASSURED

*Jesus answered them, "Do you finally believe? In fact,
you're about to make a run for it—saving your own skins
and abandoning me. But I'm not abandoned. The Father
is with me. I've told you all this so that trusting me,
you will be unshakable and assured, deeply at peace.
In this godless world you will continue to experience
difficulties. But take heart! I've conquered the world."*

JOHN 16:31–33 MSG

To think you will escape hard things in this life only sets you up for heartbreak. Being a woman of faith doesn't provide you with a free pass from fear. You will still experience countless moments filled with angst—the kind that threatens to pull you underwater. You'll face plenty of worrisome situations that can keep you up at night, pacing the floor uneasily. And sometimes you may find peace elusive and your heart anxious.

But take heart, friend! God is with you and for you. His love is unshakable. And He is fully aware of everything causing fear and worry in your life. Not only has He conquered this world with all its troubles, but He continues to conquer and will continue until you see Him face-to-face. God is constantly working on your behalf. Have the courage to let Him fight your battles.

*God, I give You all my worries. Thank You that You have
promised to be with me always. In Jesus' name I pray. Amen.*

STAY IN THE LIGHT

*Jesus once again addressed them: "I am the world's
Light. No one who follows me stumbles around in
the darkness. I provide plenty of light to live in."*
JOHN 8:12 MSG

The reality is that our world today can be dark. While we are always able to find joyful moments when we look for them, sometimes it's difficult. Between fractured relationships, heartbreaking situations, grief-filled moments, financial woes, and parenting worries, living with hope is often a struggle. And if we're not prayerful and focused on the Lord's light, fear will overshadow every area of our life until we allow it to pull us under. God wants better for us.

Anytime you feel the darkness closing in on your heart, cry out to the Lord. Put on praise and worship music. Open the Bible and read scripture out loud. Pray with fervor for God to save you from your fears. Reach out to a friend who will offer you godly wisdom and encouragement. Think back to the times God showed up in your life. These are the ways to stay in the light. And when you take these steps, He will call your intentional efforts courageous!

*God, help me remember that Your light will always trump
the world's darkness. And even more, please give me
the courage to look for it! In Jesus' name I pray. Amen.*

GOD'S KISS OF PEACE

Above the furious flood, the Enthroned One reigns,
the King-God rules with eternity at his side. This is
the one who gives his strength and might to his
people. This is the Lord giving us his kiss of peace.
PSALM 29:10–11 TPT

When your life feels tornadic and out of control, ask the Lord to calm the storm. He's above it all, sitting on a throne where confusion doesn't exist. He isn't a God of chaos. So remember when your circumstances feel that way, you don't have to. With His help, you'll be able to stand strong in life's storms rather than be tossed around by fear and anxiety.

Where do you need His kiss of peace today? Take inventory of where you're feeling stirred up. What keeps you up at night, full of worry and angst? Invite Him into those spaces right now, friend. Open your mouth and tell Him all the things weighing heavily on you. Ask God to give you strength and perspective so you can operate from a place of calm. Then wait as He infuses you with a fresh dose of courage.

God, I'm desperate for Your help. I am exhausted
from always being on point, and I'm scared my life
will never settle down. I just can't continue feeling
this way. Please bless me with Your kiss of peace.
In Jesus' name I pray. Amen.

WHEN GOD'S PATH GOES THERE

*Even when your path takes me through the valley
of deepest darkness, fear will never conquer me,
for you already have! Your authority is my strength
and my peace. The comfort of your love takes away
my fear. I'll never be lonely, for you are near.*

PSALM 23:4 TPT

Sometimes it's hard to understand why God's path takes us through dark seasons in life. We can be so quick to blame the devil in those times. We point our fingers at him for the valleys we're scraping and crawling through. But today's verse reminds us that God often intentionally takes us there as part of His beautiful plan. So how do we respond? We cling to Him.

Just as the psalmist recognized in his own journey, God promises to remain close to you. He will lead your every step because He's right there with you. The Lord knows the best route to take for His desired results. So when you bravely surrender your fears and follow His leading, strength and peace will follow. And God will be captivated by your courage.

*God, I'm surprised to know You're the One who leads me
into difficult places. Grow my faith and increase my courage
to trust You and follow Your lead. Comfort me through
each difficulty I face, Lord. In Jesus' name I pray. Amen.*

HELP IS ON THE WAY

But Yahweh, may your name be blessed and built up!
For you have answered my passionate cry for mercy.
Yahweh is my strength and my wraparound shield.
When I fully trust in you, help is on the way.
I jump for joy and burst forth with ecstatic, passionate
praise! I will sing songs of what you mean to me!
PSALM 28:6–7 TPT

Whenever you need help, God is there. Don't sit in your anguish. Don't let fear drag you down. Don't allow worry or anxiety to be the driving force in your life. Instead, trust the Lord to meet your every need because He loves you! Friend, God is your strength and shield. Let Him show you the expanse of His protection.

You don't have to suffer in silence or try to figure things out on your own. Your requests aren't restricted in number or possibility. The only requirement is offering God your complete trust, which opens the door for His help and sparks your passionate praise for His deliverance. Have the courage to trust the Lord! Let Him see your bold faith and call you brave.

God, thank You for loving me so deeply. Thank You for
always being willing to help me. Thank You for being
my strength and shield. Thank You for answering my
cries. I love You, Father! In Jesus' name I pray. Amen.

GOD IS THE LIGHT

*The people who walked in darkness have
seen a great light. They lived in a land of
shadows, but now light is shining on them.*
ISAIAH 9:2 GNT

Can you remember walking through a season of darkness? It was a time when you struggled to find joy. You couldn't hold on to peace for long. Things seemed bleak. And even when you faked a smile and went through the motions of the day, nothing good came of it. Instead, your heart was filled with fear for the future. Worry kept you up at night. And you lost hope.

It's so important we remember that God is light. In those fearful times when we're weary and anxious, He is the One who has the power to dispel the darkness that suffocates us. It's His light that brings us comfort and calms our concerns. But, friend, you have to take that brave step and pursue it. It's up to you to cry to the Lord for help. And when you do, God will call you courageous!

*God, please come close to me when I'm trying to navigate a
season of darkness. Give me hope that everything will be okay.
Help me cling to You so I don't fall into deep discouragement.
Open my eyes to see Your hand moving in my situation. Bring
me peace and comfort and shine Your precious light
into my heart. In Jesus' name I pray. Amen.*

WONDERING WHY HE CARES

I look up at your macro-skies, dark and enormous, your handmade sky-jewelry, moon and stars mounted in their settings. Then I look at my micro-self and wonder, why do you bother with us? Why take a second look our way?
PSALM 8:3–4 MSG

With all our flaws and imperfections, do you ever wonder why God gives us the time of day? We're just specks on a massive map of His beautiful creation. How could He care so much about us? Maybe you wonder why He should even bother because you'll never live a life worthy of His love. It can be a scary path to walk, thinking you're not worth His time and concern. Be careful, friend.

The truth is that you matter greatly to God. He created you on purpose and for a purpose. You're not a mistake or mishap. He wasn't in a bad mood when He thought you up. And God is delighted by your micro-self—from the top of your head to the bottom of your toes. You don't have to worry. You don't have to perform. You just have to muster the courage to embrace the truth that you're loved by the One who made you. Let Him see your confident acceptance of that precious truth!

God, thank You for loving me the way You do! In Jesus' name I pray. Amen.

WHEN YOU'RE WORRIED YOU CAN'T FINISH

*For in spite of this, my Lord himself stood with me,
empowering me to complete my ministry of preaching
to all the non-Jewish nations so they all could hear the
message and be delivered from the mouth of the lion!*
2 TIMOTHY 4:17 TPT

When you're worried you won't have the energy to complete the task before you, tell God about it. Be willing to open up and share your concerns. Be honest and truthful about what scares you. Tell the Lord the lies you're believing that are shutting you down. Unpack the disappointing outcomes and horrible endings you're predicting that are causing anxiety. Friend, just put it all out there.

Once done, ask for His help. Ask Him to infuse you with His wisdom and strength. Ask for a renewed vision for the task at hand. Ask for a huge dose of passion and purpose for what's ahead. And then trust that God will give you everything you need to finish strong. That kind of faith will delight Him, and He will call you courageous!

*God, there are so many reasons I feel too weak to complete the
work.
I am filled with worry and anxiety that I won't have the wisdom
or strength to finish it. Honestly, success just feels impossible.
Please help me. Put my fears to rest so I can trust in You. Make me
confident that I can do hard things. In Jesus' name I pray. Amen.*

PUSHED TO THE WALL

Pushed to the wall, I called to GOD; from the wide open spaces, he answered. GOD's now at my side and I'm not afraid; who would dare lay a hand on me?
PSALM 118:5–6 MSG

Can you relate to the psalmist? Chances are we've all faced times when our circumstances seem to have pushed us to the wall. They're too big for us to manage on our own, and so much fear is attached to them. No doubt it's hard to be stuck in a difficult place. In those times, what have you done? How did you find your way out? Who did you ask for help?

Our God is a jealous God, and He wants to be the One to save. He is willing and able! He's always on your side. And His rescue may come in many forms, including good friends, new revelations, open doors, or other kinds of divine intervention. He hears your every word and knows your every thought. You're not alone in your fear and frustration. Call out for His help, and He will call you courageous.

God, I feel pressed from every side. It feels like life's challenges are crushing me and I can't break free from the fear and oppression. Hear my cry and rescue me. Be present with me so I can stand up with courage. Grow my confidence in Your protection. Grow my faith in Your love. In Jesus' name I pray. Amen.

WHEN TRUSTING IS SCARY

*Lord, it is so much better to trust in you to save
me than to put my confidence in someone else.
Yes, it is so much better to trust in the Lord to
save me than to put my confidence in celebrities.*
PSALM 118:8–9 TPT

Putting our trust in others can be scary. Even though we know they love us and want the best outcome for our situation, too many times they've let us down. They haven't been available when we needed them, or their advice wasn't helpful. And in our desire to preserve the relationship, chances are we've exhausted them anyway with our emotionality. So we've learned to trust ourselves and suffer alone.

Instead, friend, let God be the One you trust. Let Him be the heavenly Father to you He has always wanted to be. Give the Lord top billing in your struggles. Unlike your friends and family, He won't falter in support and let you down. God's track record is perfect. So take a deep breath, push aside your fear, and press into your faith in the Lord. He'll see your courage and honor it!

*God, I know those around me love big and just want the best.
Yet in their humanity, they've let me down, often without even
realizing it. Let me release them from unrealistic expectations
as I place my trust in You instead. I know You'll calm every
fear and bring healing. In Jesus' name I pray. Amen.*

WHEN EVERYONE SEEMS TO BE AGAINST YOU

They pushed hard to make me fall, but the LORD helped me. The LORD is my strength and my song. He is my savior.
PSALM 118:13–14 GW

Do you ever feel ganged up on, like everyone is against you? It's a horrible feeling that causes so much anxiety and unrest. Maybe you stood up for what was right, but it wasn't the popular choice. Maybe you spoke up to advocate for someone, but it wasn't appreciated. Maybe you stepped out in a different direction, but many thought it was too disruptive to the way things usually are. Or maybe some people were setting you up for a fall, waiting to watch you fail.

It's scary to feel so alone, but you can fortify your heart by remembering that you are not. You never have been, and God promises you never will be. He is your Rescuer—the One who will help you through anything. He'll calm your fears with His love and build your confidence with His strength. And when it seems the world is against you and you run to God, He will see your grit and call you courageous.

God, I thought I was more liked than I actually am. I thought my community would stand with me no matter what. But I've learned that You're with me always. And You'll save me from myself and others. Thank You. In Jesus' name I pray. Amen.

THE POWER OF PRAISE

The LORD protects and defends me; I trust in him.
He gives me help and makes me glad;
I praise him with joyful songs.
PSALM 28:7 GNT

Have you ever lifted your voice in song to God? We probably all sing in church, or maybe we sing with our favorite Christian artist on the radio while in our car running errands. But have you ever–in fear or sadness–praised Him in song? Our worship of God in this way is a powerful weapon and one that pleases the Lord because we're actively surrendering our worries through praise.

You can praise the Lord because He protects you. You can praise Him because He defends you against enemies trying to hurt you. He is worthy of your praise because God is trustworthy and faithful. So, friend, when you're battling fear, open your mouth and sing! Sing your favorite hymn or make up your own song. Your confidence in His deliverance never goes unnoticed!

God, I struggle to break out in song when my heart is heavy.
In those times, I'm usually running low on joy and gladness.
But I can still choose to lift my voice in thanksgiving, knowing
You are with me and for me. I can sing, knowing Your heart
is full of goodness and love. In Jesus' name I pray. Amen.

BEGGING FOR HELP

I'm pleading with you, Yahweh, help me! Don't
close your ears to my cry, for you're my defender.
If you continue to remain aloof and refuse to
answer me, I might as well give up and die.
PSALM 28:1 TPT

Don't give up on your pleas to God for help. Don't be embarrassed or think that your cries for help show a lack of faith. When your worry and anxiety are off the charts and He isn't bringing immediate relief, don't be above begging for the Lord's intervention. All throughout the Bible, we see the oppressed begging for God to show up in their situation. Men terrified and tortured have pleaded with fervor.

Sometimes in our worry and pain, desperation is all we've got. We're scared of facing potentially terrible outcomes or endings. We're worried all our efforts will be for naught. We're anxious about navigating so many unknowns. In reality, begging God to show His hand in your situation reveals your level of trust. Because at the end of the day, you know He's your only hope. And it's a bold, faithful move that God calls courageous.

God, I'm desperate. If You don't show up, I have no hope
of getting through this situation. Please hear me and
help me. I need You now! In Jesus' name I pray. Amen.

DO YOU HAVE FOMO (FEAR OF MISSING OUT)?

Steep your life in God-reality, God-initiative, God-provisions. Don't worry about missing out. You'll find all your everyday human concerns will be met.
MATTHEW 6:33 MSG

In our desire to be a good Christian, we may think we have to miss out on all the fun things in life. We seem to think we can only have one or the other. We can either have a great life or follow Jesus. Why do we think walking in faith takes away the joy of living? Why are we scared to go all in with God? What do we want that a relationship with the Lord will keep us from? What are we afraid of?

This kind of mindset is dangerous. It's deflating. And it's just untrue. Being a Christian should never give you FOMO, because you're not missing out on anything. In fact, you have access to unmatched joy and favor! So go ahead and dive into the deep end with the Lord. Make your relationship with Him a priority. That choice is a courageous one, and in your spirit, you'll feel Him tell you so.

God, I want to go all in with You. I want to live sold out for Jesus. Give me the right perspective so I don't feel like a relationship with You is the consolation prize. You are the grand prize, and I want it! I love You, Lord! In Jesus' name I pray. Amen.

MADE TO SHINE

"If I make you light-bearers, you don't think I'm going to hide you under a bucket, do you? I'm putting you on a light stand. Now that I've put you there on a hilltop, on a light stand—shine! Keep open house; be generous with your lives. By opening up to others, you'll prompt people to open up with God, this generous Father in heaven."
MATTHEW 5:15–16 MSG

Sometimes it's scary to live out our faith with boldness. We worry about being judged by those around us. We're full of anxiety, concerned our choice to love Jesus might turn someone off. What if we are criticized or ridiculed in public, or labeled as something hurtful? In our fear, we have the tendency to keep that part of our life. . .*quiet.*

But, friend, God created you to shine! He made you to be an advertisement for Him with your life. He isn't expecting perfection. Instead, God wants bravery with your words and actions because they have the power to point others to the Lord above. It takes courage to live out loud, and He'll give it when you ask. And you can know that your confidence delights Him.

God, being a light feels intimidating because I am so imperfect. The responsibility feels huge. Please grow my courage so I can be intentional in the way I live. In Jesus' name I pray. Amen.

IS GOD REAL TO YOU?

I love you, Yahweh, and I'm bonded to you, my strength!
Yahweh, you're the bedrock beneath my feet, my faith-
fortress, my wonderful deliverer, my God, my rock of rescue
where none can reach me. You're the shield around me,
the mighty power that saves me, and my high place.
PSALM 18:1–2 TPT

Thankfully, we don't have to worry whether God is real. We don't have to wonder if the whole idea of faith is legit. Instead, we can take inventory of our life and earmark every time He came through. Think of the times money showed up at the last possible moment or a door opened when each one was shut a minute earlier. Remember when a hard-hearted person softened their stance toward you, or a marriage headed for divorce unexpectedly changed course? These aren't moments of good luck. This is the Lord showing Himself real.

Choose to live like you know God is alive and active not only in your life, but also in the world today. Be bold in the way you trust Him. Let faith be your guide. Remember that the Lord will call courageous those who choose to believe and walk it out as proof.

God, I know You are real. Thank You for being present
in my life every day. In Jesus' name I pray. Amen.

STRENGTHEN YOURSELF IN GOD

David and his men burst out in loud wails—wept and wept until they were exhausted with weeping. David's two wives, Ahinoam of Jezreel and Abigail widow of Nabal of Carmel, had been taken prisoner along with the rest. And suddenly David was in even worse trouble. There was talk among the men, bitter over the loss of their families, of stoning him. David strengthened himself with trust in his GOD.

1 SAMUEL 30:4-6 MSG

In today's verse, David and his men have returned to their homes only to find their families gone. They were taken while the men were gone. This unexpected discovery was a terrible moment. In their pain and anguish, the men turned their anger toward David and talked about killing him. Having no one standing with him, David had to strengthen himself in God.

Maybe you're in a similar situation where you feel alone in the battle. Where you used to have allies, now you have none. Instead, it's up to you to take the next step. This is where you stand alone, trusting that the Lord will come through. And when you do, He will call you—His beloved—courageous.

God, let my faith in You be what strengthens me today. Let me trust You first and foremost. In Jesus' name I pray. Amen.

SCARED TO FORGIVE

Tolerate the weaknesses of those in the family of faith, forgiving one another in the same way you have been graciously forgiven by Jesus Christ. If you find fault with someone, release this same gift of forgiveness to them.
COLOSSIANS 3:13 TPT

Forgiving others can be scary, especially when we believe the lies that go with it. For example, sometimes we think that extending grace to someone means what they did was okay. We think it means they're off the hook, free from any consequences. We think forgiving them invalidates our pain. And because of those fears, we're unwilling to give up our offense.

It takes grit to pardon someone who has hurt you. In our humanity, we want to cling to the pain and wave it like a flag. Sometimes we milk it for all it's worth, garnering support and sympathy along the way. But real forgiveness is fueled by the Holy Spirit. He not only gives us the willingness but also floods our heart with grace to walk it out. It's in us to forgive. And every time you choose to do so, God sees the courage it requires. And make no mistake, your forgiveness of others greatly pleases Him.

God, help me overcome the lies that often accompany this idea of forgiveness. I don't want to be in bondage from holding a grudge. Help me be brave so I can live free! In Jesus' name I pray. Amen.

COURAGE TO ASK

*I'm asking God to give you a gift from the
wealth of his glory. I pray that he would give you
inner strength and power through his Spirit.*
EPHESIANS 3:16 GW

When you're facing fear, do you ever ask God to strengthen you? It's not usually physical strength you're after, but rather the kind that comes from within. You desperately want to be brave so you can stand strong and not wilt under pressure. You need confidence to know that God is with you and won't leave you to battle alone. In your desire to be an overcomer, you crave the grit necessary to be fearless in the face of spine-weakening situations. Friend, ask the Lord for it.

Life can be hard and even scary at times, but you don't have to navigate it alone. Being worried all the time is exhausting. An anxious heart keeps you stirred up all day and brings sleepless nights. You feel alone. And often in your weakness you are tempted to give up. But when you choose instead to ask God for inner strength and power through His Holy Spirit, you'll be fully equipped for it all. Even more, that act of faith will show the Lord His daughter's courage!

*God, please give me strength and confidence to walk
out the tough situations in my life. I can't do it without
Your Spirit's help. In Jesus' name I pray. Amen.*

LET GOD BE YOUR HERO

*The LORD your God is with you. He is a hero who saves
you. He happily rejoices over you, renews you with
his love, and celebrates over you with shouts of joy.*
ZEPHANIAH 3:17 GW

Consider that sometimes our situation is bleak and intimidating on purpose. Maybe we've exhausted every avenue to no avail. We have explored every option with no relief. And in our exasperation, we are left feeling hopeless. Why would God allow this? Because when He does intervene, we will be pointed directly to His power and might and will be motivated to give the Lord undeniable victory. And why does He need us to see His hand in our circumstances? These are faith-building moments where God is the hero. They are a beautiful reminder that we are loved and seen by the One who created us.

Where do you need God to be a hero? Is it a work situation? Maybe a financial crisis? Are you lonely and struggling to find meaningful community? Maybe you're in the interviewing process for a job you really want. Regardless, take a step back and invite the Lord to be the star of your story. Find the courage to let your faith be bigger than your fear and worry. And when you do, God will call you courageous!

*God, please be the hero in my story! Help me
wait on You. In Jesus' name I pray. Amen.*

THE COURAGE TO BELIEVE GOD

*"I know what I'm doing. I have it all planned
out—plans to take care of you, not abandon you,
plans to give you the future you hope for."*
JEREMIAH 29:11 MSG

At some point, if we're going to claim to be Christian women, we'll have to take God at His word. Part of having faith means we make a choice to believe that what He says is true. So if God declares He knows what He's doing, then we muster the courage to believe it. When He says that plans for taking care of us are in place, we must decide it is truth. And because the Lord promises never to abandon us, having faith requires us to be confident in the words He speaks.

Friend, remember this when you're battling fear. Memorize today's verse so it's quick on your tongue when anxiety takes hold. Don't give worry any space in your day, especially knowing God's promise to take care of you and walk out every hard moment with you. Easy to do? No, it's not. It takes grit and determination. But it will make all the difference. Be the kind of woman who chooses to cling to the Lord's truth no matter what, and know that God sees your courage.

*God, thank You for having a plan to care
for me. Let me find rest and peace in it!
In Jesus' name I pray. Amen.*

STAY WITH GOD

*I'm sure now I'll see God's goodness in the
exuberant earth. Stay with GOD! Take heart.
Don't quit. I'll say it again: Stay with GOD.*
PSALM 27:13–14 MSG

When you feel like throwing in the towel, don't. When you want to crawl into bed and pull the covers over your head to signal defeat, stand your ground. In those moments when your faith that things will get better begins to wane, cling to His goodness. Everyone struggles with fear and insecurity from time to time. We all have moments when we want to quit or give up. And chances are we've all been frustrated with God's timing and plan. But none of that negates the truth that His heart and plan for you are always good.

The psalmist says to "stay with God," no doubt knowing from personal experience the value of doing so. There's hope for peace and safety when we remain close to the Source of all peace. But when we try to go it alone—try to walk away from God's help—we open the door for fear to take control. So the next time you're tempted to retreat, let the Lord see your confidence in Him instead.

*God, I confess I'm stubborn at times and want to
figure things out myself. The problem is that doing
so often leads to a bigger mess. Help me stay close
to You instead! In Jesus' name I pray. Amen.*

THE FEAR OF ABANDONMENT

*You've always been right there for me; don't turn your
back on me now. Don't throw me out, don't abandon
me; you've always kept the door open. My father and
mother walked out and left me, but GOD took me in.*

PSALM 27:9-10 MSG

We've all suffered abandonment by someone we thought would love us forever. Maybe it was your best friend who dumped you for a new one. Maybe it was your husband who chose to walk away without a second thought of how his actions would crush you. Maybe your mentor closed the door unexpectedly. Or maybe the abandonment that hurts you most is a parent who turned their back on you. Regardless, the fear of it happening again weighs heavy on your heart.

You can be assured—based solely in scripture—that God will never leave you. There is nothing you can do to make Him decide you're unworthy of His love or time. So, friend, let there be no reason to guard your heart from the Lord. Where you may be afraid with others, be unafraid to trust Him. That kind of faith will prompt God to call you, His beloved daughter, courageous.

*God, flood my heart with confidence in Your love
and in Your promise to stay. I need to know deep
down in the marrow of my bones that You are with me
forever and always. In Jesus' name I pray. Amen.*

KNOWING GOD IS WITH YOU

*The LORD is my light and my salvation; I will fear no one.
The LORD protects me from all danger; I will never be afraid.
When evil people attack me and try to kill me, they stumble
and fall. Even if a whole army surrounds me, I will not be
afraid; even if enemies attack me, I will still trust God.*

PSALM 27:1–3 GNT

- -

At the end of the day, God is all you really have. He promises to shine the light of His truth into the middle of your mess. He will give you courage to stand strong as you face difficult times. It's God who will protect your heart, strengthening it with bravery for the battle ahead. Too often, we look at the long road ahead or the massive mountain in our way, and it scares us. We're terrified, mainly because we feel alone, left on our own to navigate the path in front of us. But how is your heart encouraged to know that God is with you always?

This is where your faith is challenged the most. Every day you must make the deliberate choice to trust that the Lord is not only aware of your struggles but right in the middle of them. It is a choice to prioritize faith over fear, especially when your situation looks terrifying. And doing so takes great courage that delights His heart.

*God, I trust You. I know You are with me.
In Jesus' name I pray. Amen.*

IN HIS SHELTER

In the day of trouble, he will treasure me in his shelter, under the cover of his tent. He will lift me high upon a rock, out of reach from all my enemies who surround me. Triumphant now, I'll bring him my offerings of praise, singing and shouting with ecstatic joy! Yes, I will sing praises to Yahweh!

PSALM 27:5–6 TPT

Today's verse is a powerful reminder of just how protective God is of you. Maybe you feel like no one cares about your well-being. Maybe you feel as if you're all alone, hoping for support as you face the giants in your life. Few things are worse than feeling like an island, friend. So let the words from the psalmist wash over your heart right now. Remember that in the scary and tough seasons of life, God will hide you away with Him. How does that work? It's a supernatural transaction when you cling to Him in faith.

And remember the second part of today's verse that talks about your response to His protection and comfort. Let your fears be turned into praise! Have a heart of thanksgiving! Your choice to run to God takes audacity. Listen as your heavenly Father calls out your courage.

God, hide me away with You. I need to be alone in Your presence right now. In Jesus' name I pray. Amen.

WHEN FEAR IS AT YOUR HEELS

*"I leave the gift of peace with you—my peace.
Not the kind of fragile peace given by the world,
but my perfect peace. Don't yield to fear or be
troubled in your hearts—instead, be courageous!"*
JOHN 14:27 TPT

When your marriage falls apart, grab onto the peace God offers. When the doctor's diagnosis knocks you to your knees, cling to the Lord for comfort. Let Him be the One who calms your anxious heart when you discover betrayal or feel the sting of rejection. God's peace is the only kind of peace that offers exactly what you long for. It's hearty. It's sustainable. It's perfect.

You don't have to exist with fear at your heels. While some situations may incite panic or worry, those feelings don't have to rule your life. The next time something or someone sparks anxiety, go right to God. Don't waste your time looking for worldly options or trusting in your own efforts. Ask the Lord to give you peace. And when you trust Him above all else, He will call you courageous!

*God, give me the courage to trust You more than anything
else. When fear nips at my heels, give me the confidence
to ask for Your peace to calm my anxious heart. I believe in
You, and I know You will always come through to silence
the chaos and uproar! In Jesus' name I pray. Amen.*

WHEN NEWS HITS HARD

Thank you for your love, thank you for your faithfulness; most holy is your name, most holy is your Word. The moment I called out, you stepped in; you made my life large with strength.
PSALM 138:2–3 MSG

That news you received hit hard, didn't it? It was unexpected and destabilizing, causing great heartache. Maybe you knew it was coming, but nothing could have prepared you for this kind of emotional devastation. Maybe it hit out of the blue, or maybe it was the last thing you ever imagined would come to pass. Regardless, what you need right now is triage. You're hemorrhaging. This is where the Lord shines.

Never forget that God is faithful to His children. It's because of His unconditional love that He is able to meet you right where you are, in good times or bad. He is listening for you to call out for help. God's eyes are on you, looking for the signal that you need Him. Why do you tarry? Why do you try to navigate your circumstances on your own? Friend, let God be your strength. Fear cannot stand against Him. And when you invite Him into your situation, He will recognize your courage and beam with delight at His brave daughter.

God, this heartache is heavy. I'm battling fear and grief at the same time and can't come out from under them on my own. Please help me. In Jesus' name I pray. Amen.

THE POWER OF HIS WORD

God means what he says. What he says goes.
His powerful Word is sharp as a surgeon's
scalpel, cutting through everything, whether
doubt or defense, laying us open to listen and
obey. Nothing and no one can resist God's Word.
We can't get away from it—no matter what.
HEBREWS 4:12-13 MSG

Nothing will cut through lies faster than God's truth. His Word is sharp and clear for those who take the time to dig into it. The Bible has a supernatural way of giving us what we need in the moment to battle fear, insecurity, anger, hopelessness, or temptation. And no one is unaffected by it. Yes, it's that powerful.

So when you're feeling overwhelmed in life, scared of outcomes out of your control, find comfort in the Word. Turn its pages to find wisdom and discernment for the choices ahead. Let it affirm your decisions. The Bible has the answers you're looking for when it comes to standing strong through challenging and worrisome life storms, and it will encourage you in all the right ways. Don't forgo time in God's Word. Let Him see your bold belief come alive. Let the Lord see His daughter's courageous faith!

God, thank You for giving us Your Word as a guide. May it give
me confidence as I navigate this tumultuous life. May I hear
Your voice through its pages. In Jesus' name I pray. Amen.

STRONG, SAFE, AND SURE-FOOTED

*He is the God who makes me strong, who makes
my pathway safe. He makes me sure-footed as a
deer; he keeps me safe on the mountains. He trains
me for battle, so that I can use the strongest bow.*
PSALM 18:32–34 GNT

When we let fear infiltrate our heart, it will most certainly rise to the occasion. Fear isn't shy, nor does it have a conscience. If invited or allowed in, it will absolutely take up residency in the nooks and crannies of the mind. And even more, it will steal peace and destroy any joy you may have had. It makes us weak, insecure, ineffective, and faithless.

God knows fear is real and He understands how potent it can be in the lives of His children. It's part of living in a sinful world. But let's never forget that He has made a way to rise above it. In response to your worry and anxiety, God will make you strong, safe, and sure-footed. He will guide you through your fears. He will train you for battle. What's your part? Be courageous enough to grab hold of all that the Lord offers those He loves. And that includes you.

*God, thank You for standing with me through
the ups and downs of life. I'm so grateful You
promise not only to help me but to ready me for
every battle I face. In Jesus' name I pray. Amen.*

WHEN YOU DON'T
KNOW HOW TO PRAY

*And in a similar way, the Holy Spirit takes hold of us
in our human frailty to empower us in our weakness.
For example, at times we don't even know how to pray,
or know the best things to ask for. But the Holy Spirit rises
up within us to super-intercede on our behalf, pleading
to God with emotional sighs too deep for words.*

ROMANS 8:26 TPT

Sometimes we're so paralyzed in our fear, we don't even know how to pray. We can't find the words to express our worries and can't find effective ways to express what we need. We're essentially tongue-tied when it comes to our prayers to God. It's not that we don't want His help—we just don't know how to ask for it. So rather than invite Him into our anxious moments, we stay silent and hope for the best.

Take a deep breath, friend. Today's verse is an awesome reality for those times when you freeze up during prayer. Did you know the Holy Spirit speaks for you? He intercedes on your behalf, unpacking all the fear hidden in your heart. It's because of Him that God knows every detail even when you can't seem to express your situation and your needs aloud. And in response, He'll enable you to be courageous!

*God, what a relief to know the Holy Spirit
intercedes on my behalf when I can't find the
words! In Jesus' name I pray. Amen.*

HE KNOWS YOU BETTER

*He knows us far better than we know ourselves, knows
our pregnant condition, and keeps us present before
God. That's why we can be so sure that every detail in our
lives of love for God is worked into something good.*
ROMANS 8:27–28 MSG

Trust that God completely understands every bit of the fear you're feeling. Sometimes it's hard to find the right words to describe what we're battling inside. We're stirred up by emotions that we can't explain. And because we're afraid to dig deeper into the origin of those emotions, we give them free rein in our heart and mind.

Here's an amazing truth: The Lord sees you. Not only can He look deep inside the hidden places, but He sees every detail down to the smallest. Where you can't understand the ups and downs you're facing, God understands your situation completely and will turn it around for your benefit. He knows your fears and weaknesses and is working out everything for your good. He sees the boldness you exhibit in trusting Him with your heart, and He calls you courageous.

*God, I'm thankful You know me better than I know myself.
It calms my heart and keeps me from feeling panicky.
Help me rest in the truth that You're involved in every part
of my life, making sure I reap the benefits of every hard
thing I go through. In Jesus' name I pray. Amen.*

SCARED TO LOVE

Love is patient. Love is kind. Love isn't jealous.
It doesn't sing its own praises. It isn't arrogant. It isn't
rude. It doesn't think about itself. It isn't irritable.
It doesn't keep track of wrongs. It isn't happy when
injustice is done, but it is happy with the truth.
1 CORINTHIANS 13:4–6 GW

It takes courage to step out and love again, especially when we've been burned in the past. To open your heart up takes grit and determination, and a level of confidence that can come only from God. Ever worry you'll never be able to trust someone? Maybe the idea of letting another in feels reckless. Are you afraid you'll never be able to love them well because of a failed relationship in the past? Or maybe you're insecure, terrified they'll reject you.

Take those fears to God and let Him be the One to sort things out. Believe that He will honor your efforts—even the ones that may fall short at times. The idea isn't to love with perfection. Only God can do that. But when you choose to love another selflessly and with purpose, the Lord will see your determination and call you courageous for trying one more time.

God, I'm nervous to open my heart again. I'm
trusting You will help me take that next step out of
my comfort zone. In Jesus' name I pray. Amen.

THE COURAGE OF AGING

So we're not giving up. How could we! Even though on the outside it often looks like things are falling apart on us, on the inside, where God is making new life, not a day goes by without his unfolding grace. These hard times are small potatoes compared to the coming good times, the lavish celebration prepared for us. There's far more here than meets the eye. The things we see now are here today, gone tomorrow. But the things we can't see now will last forever.

2 CORINTHIANS 4:16–18 MSG

Some of us are worried about all the issues that come with aging. From aches and pains to wrinkles and sags. From forgetfulness to feebleness. From feeling irrelevant and undervalued rather than necessary and important. The truth is that aging isn't for sissies.

Here is something so worthy of remembering. Your outside may be falling apart and wearing down, but every day your insides are made new. His mercies are new every morning. So when you are afraid of the changes you're seeing, hold tight to the truth that your spirit doesn't age. It doesn't grow old. Choosing to embrace this beautiful truth will earn you the title of courageous in God's eyes.

God, help me be brave as I age. Keep me from discouragement. Give me Your perspective so I can find peace and comfort. In Jesus' name I pray. Amen.

THE COURAGE TO BE YOURSELF

*So be content with who you are, and don't
put on airs. God's strong hand is on you; he'll
promote you at the right time. Live carefree
before God; he is most careful with you.*
1 PETER 5:6–7 MSG

It takes real courage to be content with yourself, doesn't it? How quick we are to dismiss the good things about who we are, concentrating instead on the places where we feel lacking. It's not a stretch for us to focus on all we are not. And it's in that lacking that we put on airs, acting like we're better than others, smarter, more important, and the like. We create a new version of ourselves, but it's not an honest one. All because we forget that God made us on purpose and with a purpose.

Friend, never forget that the Lord's mighty hand is on you right now. He has planned out a beautiful future for your life, full of challenges and victories that will lead you toward fulfillment. That means you are freed up to be exactly who you are—stumbles, fumbles, and all. Choose to be unafraid to embrace your quirkiness. You weren't made to fit in with the world. And every time you decide to be yourself—even when doing so feels scary—God will call you a courageous one!

*God, help me trust that You've created me to be who
I am on purpose. Make me brave so I can embrace
my identity in You. In Jesus' name I pray. Amen.*

THE COURAGE TO FESS UP

*So own up to your sins to one another and pray for one
another. In the end, you may be healed. Your prayers
are powerful when they are rooted in a righteous life.*
JAMES 5:16 VOICE

One of the hardest things we must do in relationships is take responsibility for the wrongs we've committed. We have to own up to the mistakes we've made, and that requires bravery. Why? Because courage has to override our fear of being rejected. Too often we worry that if we share what we've done, our friend or loved one will walk away. We'll be abandoned by those we love the most. And so asking for courage to be open and honest is a must.

Remember, there are no divine expectations for you to be perfect. While you may be confronted with worldly expectations, God is a God of second chances. And even if your confession is met with heartache, find comfort in knowing the Lord celebrates your vulnerability. He sees the courage you showed in sharing your struggle with someone. So ask Him to calm the waters and bring hope for restoration. Ask Him to honor your bravery. And thank the Lord for His forgiveness and His promise not to hold your transgressions against you.

*God, I don't like letting people down. I worry
it will lead to rejection. Give me courage to be
honest anyway. In Jesus' name I pray. Amen.*

CONFIDENCE TO SPEAK TRUTH TO THE LOST

Brothers and sisters, if someone you know loses his way and rebels against God, pursue him in love and bring him back to the truth. Know this: If you turn a sinner back from the error of his ways, then you will rescue him from the grips of death and cover the pain and consequences of untold sins.

JAMES 5:19–20 VOICE

Do you have the courage to walk out today's verse? Given the opportunity, would you go after someone walking in the opposite direction from God? It's risky because your good intentions may not come across that way. They may angrily reject your help. Even if pursued in love, they may verbally attack you. They may remove you from their lives, unconcerned that you're left with a broken heart. It's not easy to stand up for what's right, but it's right for you to try.

Who needs your encouragement today? Who is making some bad choices that will eventually lead to their destruction? Spend time in prayer, asking for the Lord to strengthen you. Ask Him to prepare their hearts to hear truth. Ask Him to fill your mouth with the right words at the right time. Share with God your worries and fears about speaking up, and then allow Him to fill you with confidence. He will delight in your courage to love someone in such a way!

God, make me brave to do Your work! In Jesus' name I pray. Amen.

LET GOD BE THE JUDGE

*Do not complain against one another, my friends,
so that God will not judge you. The Judge is near,
ready to appear. My friends, remember the prophets
who spoke in the name of the Lord. Take them as
examples of patient endurance under suffering.*
JAMES 5:9–10 GNT

When you've been offended by someone, it's hard not to want to talk about it. When your feelings have been hurt, keeping the incident to yourself feels almost impossible. It's natural to want to unpack the details with a friend or family member. And if we're being honest, it's also normal to want to blast your pain all over social media or community circles to injure the one who injured you. But that's not God's desire.

Instead of giving in to your flesh, choose to be a woman who bravely believes that God sees the injustice. Talk to Him about the emotions and hurt feelings it conjured. Let the Lord be your confidant. When we open our mouth and complain to others, we often cross the line into sin. And that judgment of others comes right back on us, because the Lord will judge our actions. Trust that God will make your situation right. Ask for the courage to let Him.

*God, this one is hard for me. I often want to retaliate,
disguised as a desire to process a hurt with a friend. Help me
remember You've got my back. In Jesus' name I pray. Amen.*

THE COURAGE TO ENCOURAGE

He said, "Don't be afraid. You are highly respected.
Everything is alright! Be strong! Be strong!" As he
talked to me, I became stronger. I said, "Sir, tell me
what you came to say. You have strengthened me."
DANIEL 10:19 GW

Are you ever scared to be an encourager? Are you timid about sharing ideas or suggestions with those around you? Sometimes we're worried that our advice isn't as wise as the advice of others. We're nervous our best wisdom may be rejected, and we'll end up embarrassed. Maybe you regard the one needing support as smarter than you, so the idea of offering up your thoughts seems silly. But the truth is that you're brilliant. You've attended the school of hard knocks and come out stronger. You have plenty of hard-won wisdom, plenty of tools in your toolbelt. So don't shy away from speaking truth.

Consider for a moment that God allowed those difficult life experiences for a reason. It could be that they were well-planned strategies to arm you with knowledge. Maybe they were designed to birth compassion in your heart. Or perhaps they brought sharp insight and perspective. In God's economy, nothing is by chance. So, friend, don't allow fear or insecurity to keep you from speaking up in the right moment and at the right time. That kind of courage pleases the Lord!

God, thank You for equipping me. Grow my confidence
to encourage others! In Jesus' name I pray. Amen.

REPLACING THE
I-CAN-FIX-IT MINDSET

People cannot save themselves.
But with God, all things are possible.
MATTHEW 19:26 VOICE

Why does it seem we so quickly fall back into the *I-can-fix-it* mindset when things get tough? Rather than reach out for support from those who care, we go it alone. We put on the proverbial big-girl pants and march forward. We become laser-focused to tackle the issues solo. We grin and bear it. But in the end—like a hundred times before—we crash and burn. We buckle under pressure because fear overwhelms us.

In those dark times, let's not forget that God promises something powerful for us to cling to—*possibility*. That means you don't have to cave to hopelessness any longer. You don't have to fear ruin or wreckage. Instead, let His promise that all things are possible bolster your faith. And when He says all things. . .He means every single thing. Believe Him. Don't entertain despair another minute. Don't decide to walk alone. Choose today to bring God into the middle of your mess. And He will call that kind of faith courageous indeed.

God, change my mindset so I will be quick to let You into
my pain. I need hope and help, and You're the only One
who can bring it without fail. In Jesus' name I pray. Amen.

WHEN YOU'RE AFRAID TO DREAM

Never doubt God's mighty power to work in you and accomplish all this. He will achieve infinitely more than your greatest request, your most unbelievable dream, and exceed your wildest imagination! He will outdo them all, for his miraculous power constantly energizes you.
EPHESIANS 3:20 TPT

How many times has your heart leapt with hope and expectation, only to sink when you started thinking through the nuts and bolts of the plan? This is fertile ground for the enemy. It's here that your excitement is doused by his constant reminders of all the times you tried and failed. This is where he triggers your insecurities, making you question yourself, certain you pushed the envelope too far this time. This is where you feel every bit of your human condition.

But there is hope! Because when you put your faith in God, this is also where His mighty power works in you and through you. The road to your heart's desire may not be easy, but together you will "achieve infinitely more than your greatest request, your most unbelievable dream." Fear doesn't get to win when the Lord is part of your plan. Be bold in your dreams and ask Him for help every step of the way. God delights in courage fueled by faith!

God, I want to dream big with You! Give me confidence as I trust You to help make my hopes and desires a reality. In Jesus' name I pray. Amen.

NEVER TOO DIFFICULT FOR GOD

"Eternal Lord, with Your outstretched arm and Your enormous power You created the heavens and the earth. Nothing is too difficult for You."
JEREMIAH 32:17 VOICE

So many things are just too difficult for us to figure out. Amen? We don't always know how to fix a marriage that has swerved off the road and is heading into dangerous territory. We don't have the answers as to how we can effectively help a prodigal child find their way back home. We don't know how to fix our finances. If we did, the hardship we're currently facing probably would have been avoided altogether. We don't have the medical knowledge to heal the disease ravaging our body. We are limited because we are human. But the Lord isn't bound by the same limitations.

Think about it. If God literally spoke heaven and earth into existence, if He made the water and land part from one another, if He created every living being and gave order to His creation, then don't you think your marriage, child, finances, and health will be in good, capable hands if you place them there? You don't have to make yourself sick with worry and anxiety, because God has you in His sight. And when your faith becomes bold enough to ask for His help, He'll see your courage and honor it.

God, I can't do this without You. I'm sick and scared and exhausted. Please see my needs and meet me in them. In Jesus' name I pray. Amen.

WHEN YOU NEED A FRESH REMINDER

*Let the dawning day bring me revelation of
your tender, unfailing love. Give me light for
my path and teach me, for I trust in you.*
PSALM 143:8 TPT

Every morning, before your feet even hit the floor, invite God into your day. Maybe you woke up to a huge weight of worry sitting on your chest. Maybe you woke remembering the horrible fight from the night before. Maybe you woke up to grief that always feels worse in the early hours of the morning. Or maybe a rush of fear for the day ahead or heartache over the events of the day before. The enemy wants you to pack up those burdens and carry them with you, but the Lord wants you to leave them in His capable hands.

Ask God to brighten the path He has chosen for you to walk with Him. Ask for His guidance as you navigate the wasteland of a broken heart. Let the Lord refresh your mind with reminders of His immeasurable and unfailing love for you. It takes courage to choose faith over your fears, and you can be sure the Lord is pleased when you do.

*God, I give You every fear and insecurity in my heart right
now. I don't have the strength to carry them. Give me a fresh
reminder of Your unfailing love today, and show me the path
to walk so I stay in Your light. In Jesus' name I pray. Amen.*

WHEN YOU FEEL LIKE
THE WORLD IS DEVOURING YOU

You, GOD—don't put off my rescue! Hurry and help
me! Don't let them cut my throat; don't let those
mongrels devour me. If you don't show up soon,
I'm done for—gored by the bulls, meat for the lions.
PSALM 22:19-21 MSG

Today's verse paints the perfect picture of how we sometimes feel. There are days it seems as if people don't like us or are annoyed by our very existence. In moments of doubt or insecurity, we may worry that some have turned against us, deciding we're no longer worth the effort. We may even go through long seasons where we feel hated and despised by people who used to love and care. And then—though probably not too often—we experience those moments when we fear the world may devour us. In these overwhelming situations, all we have is God.

Can you remember a time like this? Maybe you're in one right now. The fear factor is off the charts. Everything is worrisome and anxious thoughts can't be kept at bay. You're facing joy-draining and spirit-weakening circumstances that feel hopeless at best. Friend, don't waste another moment. Cry out to the Lord for rescue. Tell Him of your dire straits. Be bold in your requests, knowing God sees your courage and honors it!

God, please come quick. I feel like I'm about to be
devoured. I need You. In Jesus' name I pray. Amen.

YOU NEED HIS HELP!

Then he replied, "This is the word the LORD spoke to Zerubbabel: You won't succeed by might or by power, but by my Spirit, says the LORD of Armies."
ZECHARIAH 4:6 GW

Your fear will be overcome only with God's help. Anxiety and stress are best managed by putting your faith in the Lord, trusting He is actively working in your situation. Every insecurity will find freedom when you purposefully allow God to untangle them strand by strand. Do you see the common thread? It's the Lord's intervention. We need Him to be intimately involved in removing the trip wires in our lives.

That doesn't mean you are weak and helpless. Chances are you're a strong and brilliant woman, deeply capable of navigating the day-to-day. You love others well and rely on the Lord for many things. But the fact that these struggles are still in play today means you need God's help to push through to healing and wholeness. He is the One who makes up the difference. He fills the gaps where we fall short. God is looking for courageous women. Let one of them be you!

God, sometimes I struggle to ask for help because I feel strong and capable. But the truth is that my might only goes so far. Would You please bring me to the finish line of healing? I know I can't get there without Your divine intervention. In Jesus' name I pray. Amen.

DON'T FEAR SUFFERING

And then, after your brief suffering, the God of all loving grace, who has called you to share in his eternal glory in Christ, will personally and powerfully restore you and make you stronger than ever. Yes, he will set you firmly in place and build you up.

1 PETER 5:10 TPT

Today's verse confirms something important. As much as we wish it weren't so, suffering is part of our human experience. It will happen. No one can escape it, and no amount of good behavior will keep it at bay. Consider then that if God mandates it for everyone, and since the Word tells us He works all things for good, maybe suffering is for our benefit. Maybe it teaches us to believe Him more or to make smarter decisions. Maybe it shows us why trusting Him above all else is essential to mental health. Maybe when we suffer, we emerge with a different perspective and mindset. Regardless, don't allow fear of suffering to get in the way. Hardship is inevitable. You'll face grief and heartbreak, but then something amazing will happen.

Once what was supposed to be accomplished through suffering *is* accomplished, God promises to restore you. And even more, He'll do it personally, powerfully, making you stronger than before. So, friend, boldly accept the suffering before you and trust God through it, and He will call you courageous!

God, I trust You! In Jesus' name I pray. Amen.

MUSTARD SEED-SIZED FAITH

Then the disciples came to Jesus in private and asked him, "Why couldn't we drive the demon out?" "It was because you do not have enough faith," answered Jesus. "I assure you that if you have faith as big as a mustard seed, you can say to this hill, 'Go from here to there!' and it will go. You could do anything!"

MATTHEW 17:19-20 GNT

You don't have to be an amazing pillar of faith for God to respond to you. You don't need to lace the most flowery words through your prayer. You don't have to collect hundreds of volunteer hours in your community. You don't need a seminary degree or need to have gone to a Christian school. No one in your family must work in the church, nor must you have written any faith-based books. None of these will make the Lord love you more or give you greater access to His power. What you need—according to the Word—is faith as big as a mustard seed.

Your small and growing faith matters to God. It pleases Him! He sees the baby steps you're taking to trust Him with your fears. He notices the times you ask Him to calm your anxious heart. To the Lord, your mustard seed-sized faith is powerful. Don't let anyone tell you otherwise. Small courage is still courage. And when God sees it, He calls you brave and blessed!

God, bless my baby steps! In Jesus' name I pray. Amen.

ALERT EXPECTANCY

There's more to come: We continue to shout our praise even when we're hemmed in with troubles, because we know how troubles can develop passionate patience in us, and how that patience in turn forges the tempered steel of virtue, keeping us alert for whatever God will do next. In alert expectancy such as this, we're never left feeling shortchanged. Quite the contrary— we can't round up enough containers to hold everything God generously pours into our lives through the Holy Spirit!
ROMANS 5:3–5 MSG

Whenever we're battling fear and we cry out to the Lord for relief, we enter into an alert expectancy. This posture keeps us watchful. We stand waiting with great hope. Because we choose to believe God will act on our behalf, we keep our eyes and ears trained on Him. It's a time of patience and maybe even long-suffering, but we never feel cheated. Instead, we have an underlying excitement because we know God's work will soon be revealed.

Friend, let this alert expectancy be what comforts you through the uncertainty. Cling to it with all you have. Let the hope of the Lord bring peace in the midst of anxiety. God won't leave you where you are. Help is on the way. It's a bold stance to take, but God will call you courageous for it.

God, I will wait for You with an expectant heart! I trust Your generosity and kindness in my life. In Jesus' name I pray. Amen.

AFRAID TO STEP OUT
OF DISCOURAGEMENT

*Lord, I'm fading away. I'm discouraged and
lying in the dust; revive me by your word,
just like you promised you would.*
PSALM 119:25 TPT

Sometimes this life just feels like too much. The truth is, we'll encounter miles of discouragement as we journey through this world, and hope that things will get better will seem like a far-off dream. How do you respond to despair? Many of us stick our head in the sand to try to hide from it. Some grin and bear it, unwilling to be honest about the state of their heart. Others throw epic pity parties and function from a "poor me" posture. Consider how your situation might improve if you ask God for help.

Stepping out of discouragement can be scary. Why? Because locking our heart away helps us stay safe (at least we think so). But choosing to be honest and real about how we're feeling and what we're battling always impresses God. He wants truth to reign no matter what. So when you decide you want the same and you turn from fear and insecurity to the Lord, your courage will catch His attention every time.

*God, I don't want to sit in discouragement any
longer. I'm tired of giving in to it. Revive my heart
with Your hope! In Jesus' name I pray. Amen.*

MESSING UP AND A MESSY
LIFE ARE DIFFERENT

*Lord, don't allow me to make a mess of my life, for I
cling to your commands and follow them as closely
as I can. I will run after you with delight in my heart,
for you will make me obedient to your instructions.*

PSALM 119:31–32 TPT

It's okay to make mistakes. Don't let today's verse cause alarm or discouragement over the times you've tripped up. We've all made bad choices in life. Even with the best of intentions, we've all failed miserably. The reality is that we are imperfect people living in an imperfect world with other imperfect people. How could we not expect to mess up? The psalmist isn't asking God to make him perfect. He is asking for help so he doesn't make a series of bad choices that ultimately causes great damage. See the difference?

You don't have to live in terror of making a mistake. Let go of the anxiety that comes with trying to be flawless in what you say and do. And know that God will give you the strength to make better choices that please Him. Run boldly after God, and He will make you capable of amazing obedience. That's the kind of faith that will prompt the Lord to call you a courageous woman after His own heart!

*God, I'm all in but still need Your help to live
an obedient life that glorifies You. Thank You for
giving me strength. In Jesus' name I pray. Amen.*

GOD MAKES GOOD ON HIS PROMISES

Do not forget Your promise to Your servant; through it You have given me hope. This brings me solace in the midst of my troubles: that Your word has revived me.
PSALM 119:49–50 VOICE

Don't worry. God has not forgotten His promises. Whether the ones from His Word or the ones whispered to you directly, He will make good on them both. Knowing that He will come through—even if on His own time and in His own way—fills a weary heart with hope that things will get better. It's an anchor in the storm when the waves come crashing. It's an oasis in the desert when the heat is bearing down. It's a light at the end of a long tunnel, signaling the way out.

What promises are you struggling to hold on to right now? A promise for community? A restored relationship? Open doors? A medical breakthrough? Forgiveness? Joy? Peace? Be brave as you hold on to what the Lord has guaranteed. Exhale the stress and anxiety that keep you stirred up and unable to sleep. Ask God to increase your faith, and grab onto it with all your might. He will never leave you or forsake you! And know that the Lord will see your bold choice to stand strong and believe in His words, and the result will be a proud proclamation that you are full of courage!

God, I trust in Your promises. In Jesus' name I pray. Amen.

THE COURAGE TO NOT GIVE UP

So let's not allow ourselves to get fatigued doing good.
At the right time we will harvest a good crop if we don't
give up, or quit. Right now, therefore, every time we get
the chance, let us work for the benefit of all, starting
with the people closest to us in the community of faith.
GALATIANS 6:9–10 MSG

Don't allow fear or insecurity to keep you from pushing through. God's Word says our perseverance will be rewarded. He'll bless us for not losing hope and giving up, especially when everything in us wants to. Keep working in your marriage. Keep loving that person who makes it so very difficult. Keep forgiving as you continue on your journey to healing. Push toward that goal with fervor and might. Renew your commitment every day. Don't take no for an answer unless it's from God. Endure. Persist. Carry on. Because, friend, you'll reap a harvest of goodness if you do.

This is a call to be brave. This is where confidence in God's promises comes into play in meaningful ways. Sometimes it takes everything you've got to stay focused and faithful to walk out what's before you. But when you decide to trust His plan—knowing He'll give you the tools to stand strong no matter what—the Lord will call you His courageous one.

God, give me grit to not give up! I want to harvest the
benefits of perseverance. In Jesus' name I pray. Amen.

OVERCOMING FEAR OF
SINGING HIS PRAISES

*But I will sing about your strength. In the morning I
will joyfully sing about your mercy. You have been my
stronghold and a place of safety in times of trouble.*
PSALM 59:16 GW

Have you ever lifted your voice in song to the Lord? Chances are you regularly do so at church or with your small group. Maybe you sing at the top of your lungs along with worship music in your car on the way to work or as you run errands. Maybe you blare your favorite artists while taking a shower and praise your way through. But, friend, have you ever broken into song with your own words and your own melody? Have you ever carried a tune of thanksgiving to the One who has delivered and restored you?

Worshipping the Lord in this way may seem scary. Singing solo can make you feel vulnerable. You may be embarrassed by your voice or worried someone might make fun of you. But to God, your fresh, raw worship is beautiful. He's not worried about how it sounds to the human ear. Your words don't have to rhyme or be in tune to delight Him. When you muster the courage to break out in a song of praise and gratitude, the Lord will recognize your bravery and smile.

*God, help me be confident enough to sing to You.
You're worthy of all my praise! In Jesus' name I pray. Amen.*

COURAGE TO WATCH FOR GOD

I will watch for You, for You keep me strong.
God, You are my security! My God is one step
ahead of me with His mercy; He will show me
the victory I desire over my enemies.
PSALM 59:9–10 VOICE

God wants you to watch for Him moving in your situation. He is looking for expectant faith in His people. So because you believe in the Lord, be careful to recognize that He is always at work in your life—always and without fail. Sometimes this simple trust feels disconcerting because you're banking on His help without seeing any direct results. You're choosing to believe that things are happening before there is evidence.

But the Lord is clear in His Word that your value to Him is immeasurable. His heart for you is good! And God won't leave you in distress or fear. Be bold in your faith, trusting Him with your struggles. In His glory, the Lord will meet your needs as well as keep you securely connected to Him. Your natural inclination may be to lower your head and plow through whatever life throws your way, but complete reliance on God will show Him what a courageous daughter you are.

God, I will keep watch for Your hand in my
struggles and believe You're already working
on my behalf! In Jesus' name I pray. Amen.

THE COMMAND OF COURAGE

*"Remember that I have commanded you to be determined
and confident! Do not be afraid or discouraged, for I,
the LORD your God, am with you wherever you go."*
JOSHUA 1:9 GNT

Did you realize that bravery is actually a command? Today's verse is clear. God is reminding Joshua of His directive for him to be determined and confident. Friend, this command leaves no room for doubt. If you're not living this way right now, maybe you've wrongly thought that bravery is just a suggestion. Maybe you've thought it is nothing more than a good idea. Maybe it has been a hope or a new year's resolution rather than something of vital importance. Let's not forget that courage is a mandate from God Himself.

So what if you feel weak instead? What if you aren't strong by nature? How can you be courageous when you don't feel that way? True bravery comes from God's presence in your life. When you know (and believe) God is always with you, fear will melt away. The powerful knowledge of God's abiding presence will enable you to push fear aside and cling to courage. And when you take that step of faith, your bravery will be recognized and applauded by your heavenly Father.

*God, help me press into You when I'm facing a
hardship of any kind, knowing that it's Your presence
that gives me strength and courage to take that
next right step. In Jesus' name I pray. Amen.*

ENTWINED AS ONE

Here's what I've learned through it all: Don't give up;
don't be impatient; be entwined as one with the Lord.
Be brave and courageous, and never lose hope.
Yes, keep on waiting—for he will never disappoint you!
PSALM 27:14 TPT

Can you muster a visual of what it would look like to be entwined as one with the Lord? Think about the size difference between you and the Almighty. Visualize the light that shines from Him. Imagine His might and power. With that picture in mind, think of the situation scaring you the most right now. What is it that has your heart so full of anxiety? Dig deep to discover those worries keeping you up at night these days. As you compare that worldly fear to the safety you have being tangled up with God, let His enveloping presence bring comfort.

It is that powerful connection with the Lord that fuels your bravery. Anytime fear feels overwhelming, bring back to mind the visual of being entwined with Him. Sit in the feelings of protection and care. Ask Him for hopefulness and grit. Plead for more confidence. And know that when you demonstrate this kind of faith, God will call you His courageous daughter.

God, tangle me up in Your love and protection so I feel bold
enough to persevere through the difficult moments in life.
I can do all things through You. In Jesus' name I pray. Amen.

COURAGE TO BE HONEST

The wicked are edgy with guilt, ready to run off
even when no one's after them; honest people
are relaxed and confident, bold as lions.
PROVERBS 28:1 MSG

Many of us fear being honest. We feel exposed, vulnerable to ridicule or attack for revealing what we really think or feel. What if what we say isn't popular? What if we bare our soul and someone rejects us? What if we share too much? When these are our responses to opening up, consider them red flags that we're approaching honesty from a place of fear. But when we are confident in the Lord and understand that our sense of value and worth comes from Him, we can speak from a place of courage.

If God has prompted you to share something, be assured as you do. Stand tall and strong with His strength. Let the Lord give you the right words at the right time and be prayerful throughout. Telling the truth can be scary, but in taking that fear to God, you will reap the benefits and blessings of being His child. Let Him see your courage, and you will delight His heart.

God, sometimes the prospect of being honest has
terrified me. I've shared my thoughts and feelings before
and have been burned. Strengthen me with confidence
to be able to speak with Your power backing me up.
That's all that matters. In Jesus' name I pray. Amen.

LETTING GOD LEAD

*Trust in the Lord completely, and do not rely on
your own opinions. With all your heart rely on him
to guide you, and he will lead you in every decision
you make. Become intimate with him in whatever
you do, and he will lead you wherever you go.*
PROVERBS 3:5–6 TPT

There's no reason to be afraid of the future. Actually, if we're honest, we'd agree there are countless reasons—but not if we choose to rely on God. Fear rushes at us because we're unsure if we're making the right choices. We worry we aren't smart enough or strong enough to do what's necessary. And the enemy loves to whisper in our ear, reminding us of every time we failed miserably. He loves to bring confusion and doubt. The result is a sense of unrest or downright panic.

Let today's scripture encourage you to take the fear of what lies ahead to God. Ask Him to lead. Let Him be the One who opens doors or closes them. Unpack your worries in prayer. Confess your self-sufficiency. And surrender your plans to Him, inviting Him to speak His truth into your weary heart. It isn't easy to let go of control, especially when it has been a way of life for so long. But when you do, allowing the Lord to be your guiding force, He will call you courageous.

God, I trust You. In Jesus' name I pray. Amen.

PASSING DOWN COURAGE

David also told his son Solomon, "Be strong and courageous, and do the work. Don't be afraid or terrified. The LORD God, my God, will be with you. He will not abandon you before all the work on the LORD's temple is finished."
1 CHRONICLES 28:20 GW

What a great example of passing along a generational blessing. Not only did David encourage Solomon to be fearless, but he reminded him why this way of living could be possible. He essentially called his son to a life of bold faith so that he would have the confidence to walk out the task before him. What a powerful model for us to follow.

Whether you have children of your own or are a spiritual mother to someone else's, take this responsibility seriously. Remember that children watch how you live. They watch the ways you handle stress and fear. They notice when you're strong in difficult times, and they see those moments when your fearful, human condition wins out. When you're stressed and anxious, they notice. So let them see your confidence in the Lord so they understand the power of your relationship with Him. And let God see your courage in being that kind of example.

God, I take the job of passing the torch of courage and faith to the next generation seriously. Strengthen me so I can be a model of Your promises to everyone who knows me. In Jesus' name I pray. Amen.

CONTINUOUS VICTORY

*"The time is coming, and is already here, when all of you
will be scattered, each of you to your own home, and I
will be left all alone. But I am not really alone, because
the Father is with me. I have told you this so that you will
have peace by being united to me. The world will make
you suffer. But be brave! I have defeated the world!"*

JOHN 16:32–33 GNT

Imagine how destabilized the disciples must have felt hearing these words of Jesus. They'd just learned they were going to be disconnected from the Messiah and face the kind of suffering that required bravery to get through. Everything was okay until it wasn't. Can you relate? Think back to a time when your sense of security was ripped away. Remember the fear? The tidal wave of worry? But look how Jesus brought confidence in the last part of today's passage by saying He had already defeated the world. Instant calm.

The word *defeated* comes from the Greek word *nikos*, which is also the word for "victory." The grammar used in this verse implies a continuous victory. Jesus' statement basically means this: I *have* defeated, I *am* defeating, and I *will continue* to defeat the world. With one powerful word, He removes fear. Choose today to grab onto this promise and live a courageous life anchored in victory!

*God, thank You for Your continuous victory
over my fear! In Jesus' name I pray. Amen.*

TRAINING YOUR EARS
AND EYES ON GOD

*Jesus overheard what they were talking about and said
to the leader, "Don't listen to them; just trust me."*
MARK 5:36 MSG

Sometimes we care more about what others say than what God says. In our state of worry, we put our faith and trust in the words of those family members and friends we love. Or we hang on the words of politicians or those from Hollywood, giving them more airtime than the Lord. And rather than go to God in prayer or open His Word for remedies to calm our fears, we look to the news for insight. We clamor for worldly wisdom. And it gets us into trouble.

God wants you to be bold and resolved to focus on His words over anything else. His answers may come slower than you want. His voice may be quiet. And His revealed plans may be different than you hoped for. But choosing to follow Him will quiet your fears and insecurities and instill confidence moving forward. Train your eyes and ears on the Lord, friend. And when you do, He will call you courageous indeed!

*God, help me rework my habits so I focus on You
above every other voice in my life. Grow my faith in
Your will and ways. Give me the grit to block out
everything else. In Jesus' name I pray. Amen.*

FLOWING IN AND THROUGH

Now my beloved ones, I have saved these most important truths for last: Be supernaturally infused with strength through your life-union with the Lord Jesus. Stand victorious with the force of his explosive power flowing in and through you.
EPHESIANS 6:10 TPT

Want to be brave and bold? Looking to stand strong against the curveballs life has thrown your way? Ready to feel powerful rather than cower in fear? Then dig deep with God. The Word says your relationship with Jesus is what gives you supernatural strength in your life right now. Need perseverance as you parent? Need endurance through ongoing medical treatments? Need strength to stand up for what's right? Need grit to fight the mounting discouragement? Spend time with the Lord every day.

We simply cannot navigate this life on our own—at least not well. But we still try, eventually skinning our knees as we fall. But being intentional about taking every worry, fear, and insecurity to God will unlock His power to flow in and through you. It's what will sustain you through the challenges and give you courage to stand resolved. Tell God you're all in. Let Him see your brave stance of faith!

God, thank You for blessing obedience. Thank You for supplying me with supernatural abilities. I'm so grateful Your gifts are available to those who invest in a relationship with You. What a loving Father! In Jesus' name I pray. Amen.

ARMOR UP!

*Put on God's complete set of armor provided for us,
so that you will be protected as you fight against the evil
strategies of the accuser! Your hand-to-hand combat is
not with human beings, but with the highest principalities
and authorities operating in rebellion under the heavenly
realms. For they are a powerful class of demon-gods
and evil spirits that hold this dark world in bondage.*
EPHESIANS 6:11–12 TPT

Consider today's verses with new eyes because they're a treasure trove of truth. Too often we point fingers at the one who has offended us. We're angry about their comments, hurt by their lack of care and concern, and disappointed by their apathetic responses. As a result, we point all our fury toward them. And while they must own their actions and words, we also need to consider the involvement of the "demon-gods and evil spirits that hold this dark world in bondage."

Don't be afraid to fight against this "powerful class" in God's authority. Take a stand and silence them. Remember that you're covered by the blood of Jesus, and you also have access to God's complete set of armor. Your battles are more than worldly, and when you recognize and step onto the spiritual battlefield in faith, God will call you courageous!

*God, help me embrace Your authority to stand strong
against every evil intention, yet be able to extend
grace when necessary. In Jesus' name I pray. Amen.*

THE COMMAND TO SUIT UP

*Because of this, you must wear all the armor that God
provides so you're protected as you confront the slanderer,
for you are destined for all things and will rise victorious.*
EPHESIANS 6:13 TPT

Yesterday we talked about what we're up against and how our battles are not just worldly but occur in the spiritual realm. And we were reminded of the armor God provides to keep us safe and shielded. In today's verse, we see a command. The Lord says we *must* wear this armor. Because He loves us, He protects us. Unlike the wackadoo birthday gift from your crazy aunt that you'll never use, this gift of armor is essential to a faith-filled life.

Even more, notice the end result of confidently wearing God's armor. It's victory. Friend, you were made for important things. You are destined to rise. You can be brave no matter what comes at you because the Lord has made a way to win. Where do you need victory today? What fears are you facing? Decide now that every morning you'll pray Ephesians 6 and suit up with the complete and powerful armor of God. It will fortify you with peace and wisdom as you navigate hard situations. Let the Lord see your bold courage!

*God, I accept Your gift of armor and I commit to wearing
it every day for strength and confidence. Help me live
from a place of victory! In Jesus' name I pray. Amen.*

UNAFRAID OF BAD NEWS

He is not afraid of bad news. His heart remains
secure, full of confidence in the LORD.
PSALM 112:7 GW

There are no two ways about it—bad news creates instant panic and fear. Sometimes it's because our worst nightmare came true. Sometimes it's because we didn't see an incident coming. It may even be because our heart is so invested in some*one* or some*thing* that the bad news breaks us. Regardless, we are shaken to the core. But when you rely on your faith in God to keep you grounded, you will have the ability to stand strong. Rather than feeling unsteady beneath you, your feet will stand firm on solid ground. You will remain secure. Trust will be your response.

Friend, bad news will most certainly land at your doorstep. It will poke you in the back. It will let itself into your day without a care for what's best for you. Learn to expect that life will be a bumpy ride. . .but remember that you can choose to stay buckled in with the Lord. So when you get the scary call or read the shocking email, you can feel His presence right then and there as your fear melts away. And when God sees your intentional decision not to sit in worry, He will call you brave!

God, too often fear is my default. Please give
me courage to trust You over the anxiousness
in my heart. In Jesus' name I pray. Amen.

COURAGE TO KEEP YOUR EYES ON GOD

"Do not yield to fear, for I am always near. Never turn your gaze from me, for I am your faithful God. I will infuse you with my strength and help you in every situation. I will hold you firmly with my victorious right hand."

ISAIAH 41:10 TPT

When God tells you never to turn your gaze from Him, you can be sure He gives this powerful reminder for a good reason. Keeping your eyes on God—choosing to trust Him over your fear—will keep you full of hope. It's when you sit in your anxious thoughts that worry begins to sneak in. You start obsessing over outcomes and endings that could go bad. You replay each conversation, picking apart every possible detail. You feel sorry for yourself because one more struggle has made its way in. And instead of feeling empowered by God's strength, you feel weak. What a horrible feeling of helplessness.

But there is hope! Clinging to the Lord opens the door for Him to infuse you with His power and might. It gives Him space to help you work through difficult situations. You feel held by a loving, caring Father. And as you wipe away the tears and fears, you will see victory on the horizon and know it's possible. Be courageous as you trust God, and know His heart is delighted!

God, I will keep my eyes focused on Your goodness! In Jesus' name I pray. Amen.

THEIR DOOMED ATTEMPTS

Don't be paralyzed in any way by what your opponents are doing. Your steadfast faith in the face of opposition is a sign that they are doomed and that you have been graced with God's salvation.
PHILIPPIANS 1:28 VOICE

Keep steady. Deep breath. We've all had moments when we felt like we were going to sink. We've all been terrified by situations barreling our way at ninety miles per hour. Some situations can be overwhelming, and even more so as we feel like our heart is going to beat out of our chest. We struggle to catch our breath and make sense of what's happening. Without a doubt, life has a way of destabilizing us and even paralyzing us with fear.

But let's not forget the powerful weapon we always have access to: our faith. It's what allows us to stand strong when we want to crumble. It's what straightens our spine so we can stand tall. Faith lets us speak up with confidence and advocate for what's right. It's what makes us steadfast, able to endure hardship. And even more, it lets the enemy know that his attempts to rattle us are doomed because we're backed by God. Show the Lord you trust Him by embracing the power that comes from your faith, and He will call you courageous.

God, give me grit through faith to stay strong when things seem to be falling apart. Remind me You're stronger than any opposition I might face. In Jesus' name I pray. Amen.

A PRIVILEGE AND A BURDEN

*God has given you the privilege not only to believe
in Christ but also to suffer for him. You are involved
in the same struggle that you saw me having.
Now you hear that I'm still involved in it.*

PHILIPPIANS 1:29–30 GW

Following the Lord is both a privilege and a burden. Suffering is part of the Christian walk just as much as joy is. The Word says it's an honor to experience the things Christ did while walking among us on this earth, and you can bring glory to Him through it all. Keep in mind that no matter what is happening, God sees it. He will provide every tool necessary for you to be victorious. And while you may feel scared and overwhelmed as you navigate those spine-weakening moments, He is with you. Your faith is noted.

Does this passage from Philippians give you a different view of suffering? So often we feel it's unfair, so we whine and complain about it. We throw epic pity parties and invite anyone who will come and support us. But what if you chose to see suffering as a privilege, realizing your faithfulness through it will point others to God in heaven? Adopting this perspective isn't easy, and it takes a brave soul to walk it out. But choosing this mindset will show your courageous faith, and the Lord will recognize it.

*God, thank You for the privilege of following
You! In Jesus' name I pray. Amen.*

WHEN YOU FEEL THE
WOLVES AROUND YOU

*"Now, remember, it is I who sends you out, even though
you feel vulnerable as lambs going into a pack of wolves.
So be as shrewd as snakes yet as harmless as doves."*
MATTHEW 10:16 TPT

Do you ever feel like you're out among wolves, afraid it's just a matter of time before they attack for something you say or do? Are you ever worried that your firmly-held beliefs are under assault because they don't match up with the majority view? Maybe you know the vulnerability of wading through deep waters, just waiting to be taken down. This is when we need to ask the Lord for His wisdom with each step. Friend, it's yours for the asking. No need to cower in fear when God will open your ears and eyes to His will when you ask.

Your job? Use the discernment the Lord provides to be smart as a snake while at the same time gentle as a dove, doing no wrong. You can only walk out this kind of tension with God's help. So when you begin to feel like a sheep surrounded by wolves, pray. Ask for wisdom to navigate each situation with faith and resolve. And when you rise to the occasion with courage rather than cowardice, God will call you His brave one!

*God, I need Your wisdom and discernment!
In Jesus' name I pray. Amen.*

WHEN DAY FEARS
INVADE YOUR NIGHT

*The wise counsel GOD gives when I'm awake is confirmed
by my sleeping heart. Day and night I'll stick with GOD;
I've got a good thing going and I'm not letting go.*
PSALM 16:7–8 MSG

Ever notice that when you've had a good day with the Lord—listening, praying, and praising—your night is more restful? Sleep comes easy and your slumber isn't fitful. Too often, those wee hours of the morning are when we wrestle with our fear and insecurity from the day. Be it our busy schedule or unwillingness to deal with the issues at hand, we're left to work things out in the dead of night. Rarely do we appoint those hours as the time to chew on our worries; it just happens to be the time when we are still and alone with our thoughts.

Talk to God today about the weariness of your heart. Let Him know about the anxiety you're struggling with. Be honest about what's worrying you. Share every fear that's stirring you up. And then ask His thoughts on these things. Allow Him to minister directly to those places. Let the Lord give you wisdom, peace, and confidence during the day so you can find comfort and rest at night. Be courageous in your requests—God loves a brave heart!

*God, remind me to talk to You during the day so my
nights are peaceful. In Jesus' name I pray. Amen.*

BOLD FAITH

Shadrach, Meshach, and Abednego answered,
"Your Majesty, we will not try to defend ourselves.
If the God whom we serve is able to save us from the
blazing furnace and from your power, then he will.
But even if he doesn't, Your Majesty may be sure that
we will not worship your god, and we will not bow
down to the gold statue that you have set up."
DANIEL 3:16–18 GNT

Isn't the faith of these three men beautiful? They'd been ripped from their homeland and transplanted into an unfamiliar, pagan society, all of a sudden facing death for nonconformance. What a shock to the system! Many would have tossed in the towel. Anxiety would have stripped them of courage. Fear would have driven them to give up so they could survive. But the faith of His servants Shadrach, Meshach, and Abednego was so remarkable that God decided to record it in the Bible for us. They had an "even if" kind of faith—the kind that knows He can but won't waver in belief if He chooses not to. This kind of faith is a benefit of much time spent with the Lord.

Such bold trust doesn't come by mistake. It can't be faked, especially in the face of dire circumstances. This time-tested, hard-won level of faith sets the believer apart because of its boldness. Are you bold, friend? Ask God to increase your faith to trust Him no matter what. Your courage will delight the Lord.

God, bless me with "even if" faith. In Jesus' name I pray. Amen.

THE ARMY AROUND YOU

*Hezekiah rallied the people, saying, "Be strong!
Take courage! Don't be intimidated by the king of
Assyria and his troops—there are more on our side
than on their side. He only has a bunch of mere men;
we have our GOD to help us and fight for us!"*
2 CHRONICLES 32:6–8 MSG

Few people like to be alone. Most would never choose it. And it's because God made us for community that we naturally crave fellowship with others. We want to be around others because it gives us a sense of belonging. We need an army of family and friends to help us navigate the ups and downs life brings our way. Even if our army is small, they make us brave against the giants standing before us.

Take time to thank God for your community. They are a gift! He has placed these amazing people in your life to help you be strong as you work through difficult situations. The Lord infuses them with encouragement to pass along when you need it. And they remind you God is on your side and victory is possible. You don't have to give in to fear, friend. Just look around at the army He has placed by your side. It may be small, but it is backed by His power, making it mighty indeed. Take courage and know your bravery pleases God.

*God, thank You for my army of supporters!
In Jesus' name I pray. Amen.*

TRUST WITH ALL YOUR HEART

But in the day that I'm afraid, I lay all my fears before you and trust in you with all my heart. What harm could a man bring to me? With God on my side, I will not be afraid of what comes. The roaring praises of God fill my heart as I trust his promises.

PSALM 56:3-4 TPT

What does it mean to trust God with all your heart? It sounds like a big undertaking, especially when we're not exactly sure what it entails. Maybe it means there's no room for doubt—not one ounce. Maybe it means we move from the driver's seat to the backseat, determined not to grab the wheel of control (even for a second). Maybe we refuse to cooperate with fear and worry, instead giving every anxious thought to God. Maybe we choose rest instead of flitting around trying to fix everything. Without a doubt, trust is an active and ongoing decision.

Don't miss the benefit of this posture as explained in today's verses. Did you notice fear dissipates? Did you see that praises fill every nook and cranny of your heart? Friend, with God by your side, you have nothing to fear. Trust Him fully and listen in your spirit as He calls you brave.

God, I'm choosing to put all my faith in You, believing my fears will be replaced by courage. In Jesus' name I pray. Amen.

CRAVING HIS KINDNESS

*Lord, show me your kindness and mercy, for these
men oppose and oppress me all day long. Not a day
goes by without somebody harassing me. So many
in their pride trample me under their feet.*

PSALM 56:1–2 TPT

Sometimes we just need kindness and mercy. So often we are faced with mean-spirited people and oppressive situations. We feel bullied for sharing an opinion and outcasted for going against the groupthink. People misconstrue our comment as rude or become offended by an innocent action on our part. And rather than receiving the benefit of the doubt or being offered grace for a misunderstanding, too often we find ourselves in the middle of a storm of condemnation.

When those times hit, run to God. Take every fear and heartache directly to Him and ask for comfort. Ask for His peace to rest on you. Invite Him to give you perspective and wisdom. Share your anxious thoughts in detail. Purge every worry and hurt. And wait for God to still your heart with His love and grow your confidence in Him. Let the Lord be the One to make you courageous for every battle that comes your way.

*God, sometimes life just beats me up and I am left feeling
hopeless and weak. Please grow my faith and courage so
I can stand again. Infuse me with Your strength, and stay
close beside me every day. In Jesus' name I pray. Amen.*

DO YOU FALL TO PIECES?

If you fall to pieces in a crisis, there wasn't much to you in the first place.
PROVERBS 24:10 MSG

This proverb may sound harsh, but the Word of God is often direct and challenging. And it's also written with deep love and care. So don't skip over the bold statement in this scripture. Instead, take a moment for self-reflection. When you received a difficult phone call or the doctor's report was startling, how did you respond? When your child was struggling in school or your marriage was on the rocks, how was your heart? When your best friend betrayed you or you lost a parent, how did you handle the crisis? Maybe you let fear get the best of you. Maybe it broke you into pieces and you hid away. Or maybe you ran right to the Father.

The point of today's verse is to open your eyes to the truth of your faith. Don't be discouraged, friend. Instead—based on your personal insight—readjust your focus on God. Let the Lord grow your trust in Him to increase your strength in a crisis. Deepen your relationship with Him so you truly believe He will save you. And ask for the grit to face whatever life brings your way. God will see your courage and will bless it.

God, I want to be a woman full of faith in You. Help me stand strong as I choose to trust. In Jesus' name I pray. Amen.

OVERCOMING THE FEAR
OF RESCUING OTHERS

Don't hesitate to rescue someone who is about to be executed unjustly. You may say that it is none of your business, but God knows and judges your motives. He keeps watch on you; he knows. And he will reward you according to what you do.
PROVERBS 24:11-12 GNT

Don't be afraid to stand up for someone who is innocent. Too often, people worry about the retribution they may receive for speaking up for another. And honestly, this concern is completely valid, because anger and judgement may indeed come your way. But the Lord is your Protector, and He rewards the just. Your boldness may be what brings healing to someone. It may usher in freedom. So keeping quiet—staying silent out of fear of man—just doesn't cut it. Your faith is why you can speak up with confidence.

Remember that fear doesn't come from the Lord. He doesn't author it. Instead, God will make you as brave as a lion if you ask. He will give you the nerve to confront evil and wrongdoing. He will give you the audacity to say what needs to be said. And never forget that when God sees His beloved acting in faith, He will call you courageous!

God, I worry what others may think about me if I speak up. My insecurities get triggered at the thought of angering or offending anyone. Please fill me with courage to be Your mouthpiece against injustice. In Jesus' name I pray. Amen.

THE COURAGE TO NOT JOIN IN

Do not celebrate when your enemies fall,
and do not rejoice when they trip up; or else
the Eternal will know and be upset with you,
and He will release them from His anger.
PROVERBS 24:17–18 VOICE

Groupthink is dangerous because we can easily fall prey and join in with wrong thinking. When we choose to follow the crowd without using godly discernment to examine the ideas that others are suggesting we agree with, we will find ourselves in dangerous territory. While nothing is wrong with joining a group and creating community, we have to make sure we never blindly follow others' leading. Instead, we are wise to hold our own thoughts close, protecting every belief from negative influence.

Be careful not to join in when those around you condemn someone. Don't cheer when leaders topple from their high places, even when those leaders are not godly individuals. Don't fall prey to a mob mentality and chant hurtful words or celebrate the demise of another human being. It takes courage to stand your moral ground when everyone around you is not. But remember that God is always watching, and He doesn't want you to ruin your witness. When you feel the power to stand your ground slipping away, ask God to embolden you with His strength.

God, give me courage not to join in when those around me
are harshly judging others. Instead, give me a heart to love
the unlovable just as You do. In Jesus' name I pray. Amen.

OVERCOMING THE FEAR
OF STEPPING OUT

*"Come!" answered Jesus. So Peter got out of the
boat and started walking on the water to Jesus.*
MATTHEW 14:29 GNT

Think of how difficult it must have been for Peter to push past the fear of stepping out of the boat and onto the water. He was challenged by Jesus to grab onto his faith. It's not that he didn't want to trust Jesus. It's not that he doubted Him—Peter had seen Jesus do many miracles. But no doubt he hesitated as he considered the laws of gravity, prior experiences, and his human condition. Can't we all relate? Rarely is our fear birthed from a refusal to believe in God's abilities. We know He can do anything. But even with His perfect track record in our life, we struggle with wondering if He will come through once again.

Today, let's choose to have bold faith. If we're going to err, let's err on the side of faith that believes God will continue to come through for us. Let's be willing to step out of our comfort zone and walk toward the Lord, staying above the tumultuous waters beneath us. Know that when you take a step of faith forward, God will call you courageous! And He will bless you!

*God, help me keep my eyes focused on You and not the
storm that surrounds me. You have always come through for
me, and I believe You will again! In Jesus' name I pray. Amen.*

AN INFUSED LIFE

*I pray that God, the source of all hope, will infuse
your lives with an abundance of joy and peace
in the midst of your faith so that your hope will
overflow through the power of the Holy Spirit.*
ROMANS 15:13 VOICE

Because of the unsettling events in the world today, we can assume peace is at the top of prayer lists for God's people everywhere. It doesn't take much bad news to destabilize our heart, especially when we worry about the welfare of those we love. We're afraid of what comes next, anxious about how we'll be affected, and overwhelmed by the need to navigate all the changes. And so we must ask God's Spirit to infuse our life. He is the Source of all hope—every bit of it.

Spend time today telling God what has you spooked. As you look at the world around you, what is causing this heavy anxiety to settle on you? What issues are keeping you from experiencing His abundance of joy and peace? Friend, here is the amazing thing about God: When you place your faith in Him, the weight of worry will be lifted and you will find the hope you're desperate for. It takes guts and grit to choose faith over fear. But God will see that brave decision as beautiful, and His Spirit will cause faith to overflow in your life.

God, let Your Spirit reign in me! In Jesus' name I pray. Amen.

NOTHING CAN SEPARATE

What will separate us from the love Christ has for us?
Can trouble, distress, persecution, hunger, nakedness,
danger, or violent death separate us from his love?
ROMANS 8:35 GW

Don't worry—you're secure in the Lord. When you made the decision to follow Him, the Holy Spirit was sealed in you. You can't lose your salvation. You're God's for eternity. Friend, settle that truth in your heart right now, because the enemy will do everything he can to make you second-guess its validity. Chances are the whispers have already begun.

This verse is one to cling to when you feel scared because of what you've done or said that goes against your love for Jesus. Sometimes our humanity gets the best of us and we give in to the fleshly desires that only satisfy temporarily. We make mistakes, and then shame blankets us. Fear that God will abandon us rears its ugly head. So be courageous in your faith, remembering His promise to never leave you or forsake you. Repent and then stand bold in His truth.

God, sometimes I am so wretched. I act in ways
that don't glorify You. I say things that disappoint You.
And it's that disobedience that scares me into thinking
I've sinned my way out of Your love. Please cement the
truth in my heart so I don't doubt our relationship
any longer. In Jesus' name I pray. Amen.

SEEKING HIM CONTINUALLY

Search for the LORD and his strength.
Always seek his presence.
1 CHRONICLES 16:11 GW

When everything around you feels broken, who do you call? When your heart is overwhelmed and scared, who is your go-to? In those moments when you're caught off guard by worrisome news, what do you do? Every time your marriage seems unstable, your child struggles with friendships, your finances dig deeper holes, or you lose your job, how do you process the fear and anxiety? If you're not continually seeking God through these difficulties, you're missing out on His strength and wisdom.

He needs to be your first stop—your default. Let the Lord be the One you seek for comfort. Open your Bible and pore through scripture. Unpack your situation to Him through prayer. Journal every thought that comes to mind. Worship Him through music and sermons. These bold steps of faith will set you up to receive everything you need for the battles. They will give you confidence to take the next step as you deal with each issue at hand. And God will see your courage and call it out in the heavens. Your faith will make Him proud.

God, I want You to be my Source for everything
I need. I don't want to find hope from the world.
I don't need their solutions. Remind me to go to You
first and be blessed. In Jesus' name I pray. Amen.

A PEEK INSIDE YOUR LIFE

Whatever happens, keep living your lives based on the reality of the gospel of Christ. Then when I come to see you, or hear good reports of you, I'll know that you stand united in one Spirit and one passion—celebrating together as conquerors in the faith of the gospel.
PHILIPPIANS 1:27 TPT

Let's never forget others are watching how we live. They notice how we respond to hardships. They watch us wade through bad news. They see how we handle situations that break our heart or hurt our feelings. To think that we have a right to throw temper tantrums, plot revenge, talk trash, or spew hatefulness toward others is short-sighted. It's not that we have to be perfect. But God does want us to live with purpose, anchored in our faith. Because when we do, the Lord is revealed to others. They'll want to know why we're able to handle difficulties with authority and grace.

But a word of warning. Don't get so wound up with presenting a flawless faith that you're left stressed out. That's a quick way to shut down authenticity. Instead, be willing to share your journey honestly, always coming back to God's truths. Be willing to let others see your beautiful struggle to live faithfully, and you will find freedom. The Lord will see your bold testimony and reward you with peace.

God, help my life always point to You!
In Jesus' name I pray. Amen.

IT'S WHAT COMES NEXT

That's why we live with such good cheer. You won't see us drooping our heads or dragging our feet! Cramped conditions here don't get us down. They only remind us of the spacious living conditions ahead. It's what we trust in but don't yet see that keeps us going. Do you suppose a few ruts in the road or rocks in the path are going to stop us? When the time comes, we'll be plenty ready to exchange exile for homecoming.

2 CORINTHIANS 5:6–8 MSG

Don't allow your time on planet Earth to get you down. Live with courage even when things don't turn out the way you planned. If life is harder than you thought it would be, that's okay. If you haven't found success, give yourself grace. Maybe some of your relationships haven't worked out, your health has failed, or you've battled one thing after the next. Don't let discouragement stop you.

Be the kind of woman who lives with good cheer anyway. Rather than let worry and fear creep in, remember this life is a breath. It's what comes next for the faithful that makes the heartaches of this life tolerable. You just keep going, friend. Press into the Lord for the strength and wisdom you need. With God by your side, you've got this. And when He sees your resolve, He will call you courageous!

God, I'm living for eternity and won't let this life bring me down. Lead on, Lord! In Jesus' name I pray. Amen.

THE FEAR OF BEING A LEADER

*So stand up! Helping us follow the law is
now your responsibility. Do not be afraid;
we will support your actions.*
Ezra 10:4 voice

Let's be honest—leading is scary! For some, doing so is miles out of our comfort zone. We may cower in fear and refuse to step into a place of leadership. It could be we feel unqualified to step up. Maybe we feel unworthy of holding a position of influence. Tapes of past failures could be looping in our mind, discouraging us from trying again. Or maybe we want to keep our head in the sand and act like everything will get better on its own.

What we need is a community of people to encourage us along. We need reminders we're good enough to lead. Having that kind of support breeds confidence, something we all need as we step out of what feels familiar. Ask God to surround you with the right people to strengthen you. Ask Him to grow your courage to say yes. It's when you embrace His plan through steadfast faith that He will call you brave. You can do this!

*God, the thought of being a leader terrifies me. Honestly, I
feel so inadequate. So if Your plan is for me to lead others,
please bring community and courage so I can follow Your plan.
I want my life to please You! In Jesus' name I pray. Amen.*

WHEN CAUTION IS FROM FEAR

Joshua told them, "Don't hold back. Don't be timid. Be strong! Be confident! This is what GOD will do to all your enemies when you fight them."
JOSHUA 10:25 MSG

Sometimes being cautious is wise. It's prudent to move forward with thoughtfulness and prayer, making sure we're taking the right step at the right time. It makes sense to survey the details with discernment before we act. But other times our caution is a disservice, being more of a disobedient response that allows us to stay stuck. It becomes a quick and easy excuse when we need it. Because of fear, we too often allow caution to keep us tangled in complacency. This isn't God's best for us!

Here are Joshua's words from the verse above: "Don't hold back. Don't be timid. Be strong! Be confident!" Read them aloud and let them be what moves you from inaction to action. It's okay to take the next step even when you're scared. It's okay to say yes even though you can't see the end result. Don't let fear keep you from experiencing the adventure God has in store for you. Show Him your courage and faith, and go for it!

God, I confess that the fear of the unknown unnerves me. I don't like to put myself out there without certainty. But that's not faith. So, Lord, please give me the confidence I need to follow You anywhere and everywhere. In Jesus' name I pray. Amen.

RETHINKING FEAR
OF JUDGMENT DAY

*By living in God, love has been brought to its full
expression in us so that we may fearlessly face the day of
judgment, because all that Jesus now is, so are we in this
world. Love never brings fear, for fear is always related
to punishment. But love's perfection drives the fear of
punishment far from our hearts. Whoever walks constantly
afraid of punishment has not reached love's perfection.*

1 JOHN 4:17–18 TPT

Many fear the day of judgment because we worry what that means for us. We worry what God will say. Have we been good enough? Done enough? Did we do too much bad stuff? But, friend, since God's love has been made perfect in us, we have no need to fear that day. We can be unafraid because we have been saved from punishment through Jesus.

So the next time you find yourself anxious about that moment in time, ask God to remind you of His love. When you start fretting about the future or eternity or anything else, remember that the Lord's love drives any fear far from our heart. His love has an extraordinary way of quieting every worry and anxious thought. Choose to walk boldly in the freedom of God's love and know He is proud of your decision.

*God, help me rethink my fear and instead embrace the
love You so graciously offer me. Thank You for saving
me from punishment. In Jesus' name I pray. Amen.*

STRENGTH FOR OTHERS

*"Be strong! Let's prove ourselves strong for
our people and for the cities of our God, and
the LORD will do what he considers right."*

2 SAMUEL 10:12 GW

God tells us countless times in His Word to be strong. We're not only to be strong in our own situations but also to show strength for others. Think about it. Our kids need to see our strength because it helps them feel secure. Our parents need to know we're strong enough to help them navigate their aging process. We have to be strong when our spouse is struggling and needs to feel supported. Our strength is needed in business. It's needed in government. It's needed in community. And it's needed in the church.

So what do you do when you don't feel strong? What about the times you lack courage? How do you present a brave front when you don't feel brave inside? Let us never forget this kind of strength comes from God. We only have so much on any given day, but the Lord's power through us is formidable. He always makes up the difference! So ask God to strengthen you for the day, knowing that your boldness will delight His heart.

*God, I usually feel more scared than I do strong. I trust
You to give me the strength and courage I need to be a
stabilizing force for those I love. In Jesus' name I pray. Amen.*

YOU ARE A WARRIOR

*Then GOD commanded Joshua son of Nun
saying, "Be strong. Take courage. You will lead
the People of Israel into the land I promised to
give them. And I'll be right there with you."*
DEUTERONOMY 31:23 MSG

Sometimes we need solid reminders that God is with us. So often we feel as if we're wading through life all alone. Trying to navigate life's challenges can be lonely and scary, especially when others are depending on us. But courage is a command, and God can command it because He knows His presence will make it possible. Do *you*?

Where is the Lord asking you to be strong and take courage? Are you reeling from a doctor's report? Are you grieving the loss of someone you love? Did you discover a betrayal? Did a sure thing fail? Is a hard conversation right around the corner? Are you set to testify? Is it time to speak up? Friend, find comfort knowing God will be with you through the whole thing, giving you courage and confidence to stand strong. You are a warrior because He will make you brave. Show God you trust Him.

*God, I know that with You I can be strong and take
courage. Thank You for not expecting me to stand alone.
I love You and trust You, and I am so grateful You always
come through for me! In Jesus' name I pray. Amen.*

FAITH LIKE CALEB'S

Caleb told the people to be quiet and listen to Moses.
Caleb said, "Let's go now and take possession of the
land. We should be more than able to conquer it."
But the men who had gone with him said, "We can't
attack those people! They're too strong for us!"
NUMBERS 13:30–31 GW

Caleb saw the same people living in the Promised Land as the men who went with him. He saw their size, demeanor, weapons, and abilities just like the others. Yet Caleb obviously was focused on something the others were not—God's promise. He knew this was the exact land the Lord had determined would be home for the Israelites. His faith squashed fear because he knew God was bigger than any giant living in Canaan.

Let's have faith like Caleb's. Let's dwell not only on the magnificence of God but also on the fact that He does what He says He'll do. We have no reason to fear when the Lord is involved, but sometimes fear shows up nonetheless. When it does, ask God to make you brave as you trust Him. Ask for confidence to take the next step. And as you do, He will call courageous every choice to believe Him over your anxiousness.

God, when fear comes, let me rise above it as I trust You
instead. You will be faithful to deliver me into the promises
You've already determined for me. In Jesus' name I pray. Amen.

SPEAK UP

"Don't be bluffed into silence by the threats of bullies. There's nothing they can do to your soul, your core being. Save your fear for God, who holds your entire life—body and soul—in his hands."
MATTHEW 10:28 MSG

Have you ever felt like people just wanted you to keep your mouth shut? In their view, your thoughts and opinions were unnecessary in that moment. No one wanted your advice. No one wanted to hear your hard-won wisdom. Instead, you were bullied into silence. And because their insults became tangled with your insecurities, you allowed them to make that decision for you. Rather than speak up for what was right or speak out and advocate for yourself or others, you said nothing. Your fear of man won out.

God doesn't want this for you, friend. He gave you a voice for a reason. You have life experience to share that will encourage those around you. Your testimony helps others trust God at crucial moments in their lives. You're called to defend those who can't defend themselves. Don't allow fear or intimidation to shut you up. Respect more the call the Lord has placed on your life, and let nothing interfere with it. Remember, God will protect you as you obey. He sees you and loves you. So show Him your courage to stand strong and speak as He leads.

God, You gave me a voice for reason. Give me the courage to use it. In Jesus' name I pray. Amen.

GOD IS YOUR TRUE NORTH

*When David's time to die approached, he charged his son
Solomon, saying, "I'm about to go the way of all the earth,
but you—be strong; show what you're made of! Do what
GOD tells you. Walk in the paths he shows you: Follow the
life-map absolutely, keep an eye out for the signposts, his
course for life set out in the revelation to Moses; then you'll
get on well in whatever you do and wherever you go."*

1 KINGS 2:1-3 MSG

When our spiritual mentors leave us—for whatever reason—the loss can
sometimes shut us down. We were so dependent on them, and their
absence leaves a gaping hole in our heart. And rather than continue
moving forward in our faith and calling, we come to a standstill, feeling
lost and hopeless. We give in to despair. But let that be a red flag that
we were putting our hope in the wrong place.

Before he died, David was sure to tell his son to continue following
God because He is the focus. That advice kept Solomon steady (at least
for a while) and pointed him in the right direction. We need that same
reminder. What a gift we've been given to have mentors as guides,
but God is always our true North. So don't be anxious when a mentor
leaves, because the Lord is your lead. Have the courage to place your
faith in Him alone.

*God, I will follow Your lead above all else.
In Jesus' name I pray. Amen.*

FIRMLY PLANTED

*My dear brothers and sisters, stay firmly
planted—be unshakable—do many good works
in the name of God, and know that all your
labor is not for nothing when it is for God.*
1 Corinthians 15:58 voice

What do you think it means to be firmly planted? Consider it means being so secure in your faith in God that while the winds of fear may blow, you stay rooted. Your faith has gone deep, anchoring you to the Lord. The truth is that we can't avoid the storms that come with living on planet Earth. They are plentiful and scary at times. But scripture encourages us to dig in deep with God.

Are you firmly planted, friend? Have you weathered storms that easily could have uprooted you and blown you down the road? Or do you feel as if you're being tossed around relentlessly? Relationship struggles, financial fears, health scares, parenting stress, and personal insecurities are destabilizing at best. And sometimes they expose our shallow roots. Ask for help to sink your roots deep with God so you stay firmly planted, and know He sees your brave choice.

*God, I want to be the kind of woman who stays
steady through the storms of life. Help me
grow in my relationship with You, learning to
trust that You will protect and care for me in
every way. In Jesus' name I pray. Amen.*

COURAGE TO ASK FOR WHAT YOU NEED

So a prominent Jewish leader named Joseph, from the village of Ramah, courageously went to see Pilate and begged to have custody of the body of Jesus. Joseph was a highly regarded member of the Jewish council and a follower of Jesus who was eagerly awaiting the kingdom of God.

MARK 15:43 TPT

It takes courage to face someone intimidating. And it takes even more courage to ask them for something that might cause issues. Maybe it's their unpredictable response that's unnerving. Maybe it's the nature of the request that feels worrisome. Or maybe it's your insecurities that bring so much doubt and fear into the equation. These are the times and situations where we need God to fill us with boldness and confidence.

Who are the people who make you nervous? Who intimidates you into silence? What keeps you from asking for the raise, the apology, the help, the validation, the answers, or the commitment? What you need matters. Don't let fear stop you. Ask God to build up your confidence in Him to make every request with courage. Your boldness will delight the Lord!

God, sometimes I hesitate to ask for what I need and want. Help me find the gumption to make bold requests rather than feeling afraid to make my needs known. In Jesus' name I pray. Amen.

MONEY CAN'T SAVE YOU

*Don't be obsessed with money but live content with
what you have, for you always have God's presence.
For hasn't he promised you, "I will never leave you,
never! And I will not loosen my grip on your life!"*
HEBREWS 13:5 TPT

Sometimes in our fear, we use money as a crutch. We see it as a savior of sorts, deciding the more we have the safer we are. We hold on to it with all our might and focus our attention on getting more. And it's that obsession that leads us down the wrong path. We can't serve both God and money, which is where the dilemma begins. Too often we put money before God.

When you feel scared, run straight to God because He has what it takes to save you. He can exchange your fear for His peace. He always brings the right perspective to calm your nerves. Money only brings false hope to the hopeless because it can be gone at a moment's notice. Don't let it be what you grab for when you're scared. And know that when you cry out to the Lord for help instead, He will call your choice a courageous one!

*God, give me the confidence to take my eyes
off money and look to You as my only Savior.
You're all I need! In Jesus' name I pray. Amen.*

KNOWING GOD IS FOR
YOU REMOVES FEAR

So we can say with great confidence:
"I know the Lord is for me and I will never
be afraid of what people may do to me!"
HEBREWS 13:6 TPT

We've all been hurt by those we care about. Sometimes it's on accident, like when we feel left out or offended by something said. But other times the wound is very intentional, and it makes us afraid to open our heart again. It may have been a husband's betrayal, mean-spirited words, or rejection from a friend. Regardless, we build a big wall around our heart in hopes of protecting ourselves from another emotional injury. In our fear, we close ourselves off from community.

This is where God brings unmatched peace. We don't have to fear heartache because we know it will come. Scripture says we will have pain and sorrow. But what makes the difference is the choice to cling to God for safety through it. We run to Him when our feelings are hurt. We remember His presence means we don't have to be afraid. Let Him see your brave choice and know He will bless it.

God, I've been hurt so many times in the past that I
have closed myself off from meaningful community.
But in doing so, I've forgotten that since You're for
me, I don't have to live in fear of what others may do
to me. Thank You! In Jesus' name I pray. Amen.

GUTS TO DO THE HARD THINGS

Esther sent back her answer to Mordecai: "Go and get all the Jews living in Susa together. Fast for me. Don't eat or drink for three days, either day or night. I and my maids will fast with you. If you will do this, I'll go to the king, even though it's forbidden. If I die, I die."

ESTHER 4:15–16 MSG

What a blessing for God to include Esther's story in the Bible. He knew we'd need encouragement to do the hard things set before us, and Esther fills that role beautifully. She was so gutsy, willing to risk it all to walk out the call on her life. She never let fear get the best of her. Instead, she straightened her spine, took a deep breath, and trusted God. She knew this was her time in history to take a stand.

We may not be required to save an entire people, but sometimes things are asked of us that stir up anxiety. We're called to speak up or speak out, and stress is our immediate reaction. We worry about the hard conversations that must happen. So when God sees you stand strong in your faith and do the hard thing, He calls you courageous! He understands the faith you had to demonstrate. He knows the lies you had to overcome. And He beams with pride that you didn't let fear keep you down.

God, give me courage to do the hard things! In Jesus' name I pray. Amen.

BE CONSUMED WITH GOD

Perfect, absolute peace surrounds those whose imaginations are consumed with you; they confidently trust in you.
ISAIAH 26:3 TPT

Think about it. If your thoughts are consumed with God and His goodness, nothing else will fit. No space will be left for you to entertain fear. You won't be able to include worry. Anxiety won't have room to squeeze in. What a powerful visual!

So when your child is struggling to make friends, focus on God's promise to rescue. When your parent is showing signs of dementia, think on His promise of eternity. When you are longing to find meaningful community, remember the Lord made you for relationship. Friend, anything that stirs up fear needs to be pushed out by faith. The only things that should consume you are God's promises. You have authority over your thoughts—every single one of them. You can control where you focus your mind. Ask the Lord for help and watch Him answer. Yes, you'll need grit and determination to stay locked on God when fear comes knocking. But when you do, God will recognize your courageous stance and perfect peace will be your reward.

God, help me keep my thoughts consumed with Your goodness, because when they're not, I'm filled with fear and anxiety. I can't live with these any longer. They destabilize my heart. Instead, I want the absolute peace You offer. In Jesus' name I pray. Amen.

THE POWER OF FRIENDSHIP

*When the believers were alerted we were coming,
they came out to meet us at the Forum of Appius while
we were still a great distance from Rome. Another group
met us at the Three Taverns. When Paul saw the believers,
his heart was greatly encouraged and he thanked God.*
ACTS 28:15 TPT

Nothing beats the encouragement of good friends when we're facing hard times. Can you remember the feeling of relief when your bestie showed up during a crisis? When you were struggling in your marriage, didn't your friends urge you to stay strong? Chances are your friends delivered meals, cleaned your home, picked up the kids, or helped in other ways after surgery. And in those moments of fear, aren't they the ones you call to process the issue? Without a doubt, community makes all the difference in your life.

The problem is that we forget. So often when something hard hits, we hide out and try to weather the storm alone. We don't reach out because we don't want to inconvenience anyone. We're worried we'll exhaust them. But God included this account in the Bible on purpose, as a reminder. Find the courage to ask for help, and know that this brave decision delights God.

*God, thank You for community. Help me overcome the fear of
inviting others into my mess. In Jesus' name I pray. Amen.*

WHEN WE NEED A
REMINDER OF GOD'S LOVE

*He said, "God loves you, so don't let anything
worry you or frighten you." When he had said this,
I felt even stronger and said, "Sir, tell me what
you have to say. You have made me feel better."*
DANIEL 10:19 GNT

Sometimes we just need to be reminded that God loves us. We worry we've done the one thing He can't forgive. We worry we've sinned too often or too badly for any kind of redemption. We're concerned our whining has caused God to turn away or that we've exhausted Him by asking for the same thing over and over. We may even think He's angry, ready for us to put on our big-girl pants and figure out our own life. Friend, none of that is true. Not one verse in the Bible will back up those fears.

Let go of your anxiety right now. Ask God to speak into those vulnerable places and encourage your heart to know the truth. Invite God into your worried thoughts and let Him reveal and heal every lie you're believing. It takes courage to admit your fear and even more to ask for help. But when you show that kind of bravery, the Lord will notice and honor your request.

*God, please speak to me with kindness and help me know deep
in my heart that You love me. In Jesus' name I pray. Amen.*

STRENGTH BACKED BY GOD

"Be strong! Let's prove ourselves strong for our people and for the cities of our God, and the LORD will do what he considers right."
1 CHRONICLES 19:13 GW

There's something powerful about presenting a strong front. Strength is beautiful when it's backed by the Lord. It's confidence that stands strong while encouraging others to do the same. It's a boldness that boosts the morale of those around you. And it can settle frayed nerves and create a deeper assurance. But it's almost impossible to pull off when fear is in the mix.

The truth is, a lot of things can scare us, so unless we rely on the Lord for strength, we will cower to those fears. We can only act brave for so long. We have a limited amount of grit on our own. But every time we ask God to strengthen us, He will. And that strength will benefit and bless those around us. Even more, the Lord will see your faith in Him and call you His courageous one.

God, I don't feel strong right now. Actually, I feel weak and scared. Sometimes this life chews me up and spits me out. Please strengthen me. I have reached my human limit and can't find the courage to stand up to the struggles I'm facing. I need You, Lord. In Jesus' name I pray. Amen.

FILLING THE BIG SHOES

*After the death of the LORD's servant Moses, the LORD
said to Moses' assistant Joshua, son of Nun, "My servant
Moses is dead. Now you and all these people must
cross the Jordan River into the land that I am going to
give the people of Israel. I will give you every place
on which you set foot, as I promised Moses."*
JOSHUA 1:1-3 GW

Trying to fill the big shoes left by someone else can be scary, especially when the person who wore those shoes was loved and cherished by many. Imagine how Joshua must have felt when God tapped him to carry on after Moses' death. This man of God had played an important part in the people's deliverance. Do you think Joshua—even for a moment—felt scared to take over? But notice that right on the heels of the commission, God made a promise.

Where is God asking you to step up? Where are you being called into a leadership position? Who is looking to you for guidance and answers? Take every doubt to God. Let Him know the fear you're struggling with. Ask Him to reveal His promise. And then take courage and follow the Lord's leading. He will bless your bravery!

*God, I'm scared to be seen as a leader. What if I mess up?
Please give me confidence to be the woman You're
asking me to be. In Jesus' name I pray. Amen.*

DETERMINATION

"Be determined and confident, for you will be the leader of these people as they occupy this land which I promised their ancestors. Just be determined, be confident; and make sure that you obey the whole Law that my servant Moses gave you. Do not neglect any part of it and you will succeed wherever you go."

JOSHUA 1:6–7 GNT

Determination and fear seem like opposites. Think about it. When we're scared or full of worry, that's when our determination wavers most. That's when we want to quit. Anxiety often shuts us down, making us ineffective as we try to pursue something important. But rest assured that God knows what does fit well with determination: a generous measure of confidence. And when you ask, He will give it to you in spades.

Step out of fear, friend! With God's help, you can be strong-minded through every situation. You can persevere with grit no matter what you're up against. You can resolve to live a powerful life of faith over fear. But you need God's help. So ask Him today. And when you do, He will call you courageous.

God, fill me with determination and confidence. Make me strong in You so I don't live a cowardly, ineffective life. I need Your help to be the woman You created me to be! In Jesus' name I pray. Amen.

THE COURAGE TO FOLLOW

They answered Joshua, "We will do everything you have told us and will go anywhere you send us. We will obey you, just as we always obeyed Moses, and may the LORD your God be with you as he was with Moses! Whoever questions your authority or disobeys any of your orders will be put to death. Be determined and confident!"
JOSHUA 1:16–18 GNT

Just as it takes courage to be a leader, it takes courage to be the one who follows. Why? Because it's a humble approach that doesn't always come easily. We may not like the position of number two. We may not like to be out of the spotlight. And we may fear being unseen when we're used to being the one others look to for answers. But rather than allowing worry to overtake us, what if we chose instead to embrace the idea of letting someone else lead?

Let's be confident enough to take a step back while others rise. Let's trust that God is elevating them for a good reason. Let's be secure enough in our position with God to obey His leading in this situation. God hasn't forsaken us. We're not forgotten. Willingly submitting to authority when asked shows the Lord your unshakable faith. And He will call you courageous for it.

God, grow in me the grace and grit to follow. In Jesus' name I pray. Amen.

GOD IS YOUR STRONG, SAFE, AND SECURE PLACE

There is only one strong, safe, and secure place for me; it's in God alone who gives me strength for the battle. He's my shelter of love and my fortress of faith, who wraps himself around me as a secure shield.
PSALM 144:1–2 TPT

We may think our spouse is the one to keep us safe. Our hope may be in our parents or other adults we've known since childhood. Maybe we trust our church leaders or government officials. Maybe overeating or retail therapy gives us a feeling of security. Or perhaps a best friend or coworker brings us a sense of calm or stability. But the truth is that there is only one strong, safe, and secure place. . .and it's in God alone.

Let Him be the One you run to. Make the Lord your shelter and fortress. Look to Him to shield you in troubled times. It takes courage to put your faith before your fear. It takes bravery to trust God over earthly offerings. But every time you do, He promises strength for the battles you're facing. He will provide you with all you need to weather the storms. Recognize Him as your Savior, and know He will call you courageous!

God, You are my strong, safe, and secure place! Let it be! In Jesus' name I pray. Amen.

OVERWHELMED BY EVIL

*Reach down from your heavens and rescue me from
this hell and deliver me from these dark powers.
They speak nothing but lies; their words are pure
deceit. Nothing they say can ever be trusted.*

PSALM 144:7–8 TPT

Sometimes we feel completely overwhelmed by evil. It might show itself in the hurtful words of a mean-spirited acquaintance or even a stranger. It could be in the guise of a joy-draining situation with no relief in sight. It might arrive in the form of rejection from friends or an epic betrayal we never saw coming. Regardless, we've all experienced these dark powers that try to surround us and discourage us every day. That's why we need the Lord. He can bring perspective and comfort in those painful moments. We can have faith in His love for us.

To have faith means we trust God more than our scary circumstances. It means we don't let the weight of our worries pile up. It means we know the Word of God and choose to believe it over the lies whispered in our ear. And it means we intentionally rely on the Lord because we know He is the only One we can fully trust to care for our heart. When you choose to reach out to God rather than hide from the battles raging around you, the Lord will see your bold stance and call it brave.

*God, I know Your heart for me is always good. Thank
You for loving me! In Jesus' name I pray. Amen.*

THE PAIN OF GOSSIP

Rescue me from the enemy sword, release me from the
grip of those barbarians who lie through their teeth,
who shake your hand then knife you in the back.

PSALM 144:11 MSG

Few things hurt worse than discovering that someone you trusted has lied about you behind your back. Hearing their hurtful accusations or slander can be devastating. Not only does the backstabbing cause substantial pain in the moment, but its effects are far-reaching. Sometimes it keeps us from trusting others because we don't want to be hurt again. We are terrified to open our heart to another.

But since God created us for community, barricading ourselves from new relationships can't be the answer. And because God's Word clearly says that pain and sorrow will be part of life, we can't live in fear of heartache. So the answer must lie with God. Let Him be the One who rescues and restores. Right now, ask the Lord to remove the pain from the gossip or malicious talk and reset your heart. This bold request won't go unnoticed, and God will call it courageous.

God, my feelings are hurt and I'm battling anger. I can't believe
the things being said about me by those I trusted. I want to
either lash out or hide away, but I know neither of those is the
right option. Instead, please remove the pain and reset my
heart. I can't do this without You. In Jesus' name I pray. Amen.

FEAR ON THE HOME FRONT

*Make our sons in their prime like sturdy oak trees,
our daughters as shapely and bright as fields of
wildflowers. Fill our barns with great harvest, fill our
fields with huge flocks; protect us from invasion
and exile—eliminate the crime in our streets.*
PSALM 144:12–14 MSG

- -

We love our families. Few things can knock us to our knees like our fears related to the people inside the four walls of our home. When our kids hurt, we hurt. When our husband struggles, we struggle. In those seasons when money is tight, we worry how it will affect our ability to take care of everyone. With all of the unrest in the world, we feel anxious every time our loved ones leave the safety of home. This kind of fear strikes deep in our soul.

Make it a daily—sometimes even an hourly—habit to pray over your family. Pray specifically and by name. Pray over your finances. Pray for safety. Ask God to calm your anxious heart so you can live in peace every day. It takes courage to lay down your fear when it comes to the home front. It's a bold move that requires deeply rooted faith. Doing so shows the Lord your confidence in Him, and He will reward it.

*God, my greatest fears concern my family and
home. Replace those fears with peace as I trust that
You are in control. In Jesus' name I pray. Amen*

GIVING GOD YOUR
WORRIES AND STRESS

*If you bow low in God's awesome presence, he will
eventually exalt you as you leave the timing in his hands.
Pour out all your worries and stress upon him and leave
them there, for he always tenderly cares for you.*

1 PETER 5:6–7 TPT

We don't normally struggle to pour out our worries and stressors to God. We can spew out our frustrations without a second thought. Even when we can't find the perfect words, our grunts and groans are fully understandable to the Lord. For many of us, we know He is a safe place to unload our worries. We know there is freedom in unpacking our anxious thoughts through prayer. But the challenge comes when we're asked to leave them in His hands. It's not easy to let them stay with God, because our circumstances are quick to prompt us to grab them back.

Maybe a memory was sparked, and the worry came back. Maybe we learned additional information about the stressful situation. Maybe we became impatient waiting on God to fix the problem. But somewhere along the way, we took the fear back. Every time that happens, friend, remember to humbly return your fears back to Him. God is always ready to take them from you, without hesitation. Be brave, friend! Trust the Lord with every care and concern. Let Him see your courageous choice to have faith!

*God, today I humbly give You the worries in my heart. I trust
You to bring healing and hope. In Jesus' name I pray. Amen.*

YOU'RE NOT ALONE

Be well balanced and always alert, because your enemy, the devil, roams around incessantly, like a roaring lion looking for its prey to devour. Take a decisive stand against him and resist his every attack with strong, vigorous faith. For you know that your believing brothers and sisters around the world are experiencing the same kinds of troubles you endure.

1 PETER 5:8–9 TPT

In this world, we all need to be on high alert. We need to watch for the enemy's arrows pointed in our direction. We have to keep our eyes open and our focus steady. And when an attack comes our way, we should take an immediate stand against it through prayer. We shouldn't give in to fear but instead use divine discernment so we are ready to make a response rooted in faith.

Remember that you're not alone. You're not the only one battling hard things. Be encouraged knowing others are fighting the good fight as well. Around the world, a battle is being waged against evil. And what unites you with them isn't fear but rather faith in God. Don't allow the fiery darts to discourage you but instead to fuel your courage to stand strong and prevail. Show the Lord that He created a brave warrior in you!

God, I trust You to equip me with every weapon I need to battle the enemy before me. Together, we are undefeatable. In Jesus' name I pray. Amen.

THANKING GOD FOR
THE VICTORY

Thank God that he gives us the victory
through our Lord Jesus Christ.
1 CORINTHIANS 15:57 GW

You may be quick to ask God for help when you're feeling scared and overwhelmed, but do you circle back around to thank Him for helping? Do you acknowledge the part God played in your healing? Do you recognize the peaceful rest that replaced the sleepless nights? Have you taken time to give Him the glory for restoring your marriage or bringing the prodigal home? Does He get the credit for calming the tumultuous storms that have come your way? Let's not forget to thank the Lord for giving the victory.

It's important to have an attitude of gratitude for all God has done to dispel our fears. Taking a moment to thank Him for His hand in our life keeps our focus in the right place. We may be capable women, but God is the One who delivers us from all that frightens us. He frees us from panic and doubt and enables us to stand in courage. Where has God brought victory in your life? Today, stand in boldness and thank Him.

God, forgive me for all the times I never thanked You
for helping me. I do recognize Your hand in my life,
and I am grateful for it! In Jesus' name I pray. Amen.

FEAR OF NEVER
BEING GOOD ENOUGH

And you did not receive the "spirit of religious duty,"
leading you back into the fear of never being good enough.
But you have received the "Spirit of full acceptance,"
enfolding you into the family of God. And you will never feel
orphaned, for as he rises up within us, our spirits join him
in saying the words of tender affection, "Beloved Father!"

ROMANS 8:15 TPT

Let's remember that when we feel like we're not good enough, that perception is not from God. He isn't waiting to condemn His children. He isn't legalistic, keeping track of what we do or don't do on some proverbial chart. No. He is the God of full acceptance and folds you into His family to demonstrate it. Friend, in His eyes you are more than enough. He wants you to know that you belong–that you are a valuable part of the family.

Where do you feel unloved right now? Where do you feel like you don't measure up? Don't sit in those fears any longer, because they simply aren't true. God's creation of you was a thoughtful process. He spent time thinking you up. You are a treasure to Him. So find the confidence to grab hold of this truth and let the Lord see His courageous daughter rise up in bold beauty.

God, quiet the voices that say I'm not enough. Let me
hear Your voice instead! In Jesus' name I pray. Amen.

PRAYERS THAT
SHAKE THE GROUND

They finished their prayer, and immediately the whole place where they had gathered began to shake. All the disciples were filled with the Holy Spirit, and they began speaking God's message with courageous confidence.
ACTS 4:31 VOICE

Go ahead and pray bold prayers. You're invited to pray brave, audacious prayers to God. Ask for the big stuff—the stuff that feels impossible. Maybe it's the dream job that seems out of reach or a windfall of cash to cover mounting medical bills. Maybe it's the resurrection of a dead marriage where all hope is lost. Don't be afraid to ask for the desires of your heart, like the miraculous healing of your child's illness. Pray the kind of prayers that would shake the ground beneath you when done.

While God knows everything you're thinking and feeling, He wants to hear from you. He isn't looking for small, safe prayers. You don't have to limit yourself to ask for bite-sized bits of help. Instead, be daring and reach for the stars, confidently sharing with God the big requests too. Have the courage to pray gutsy prayers that shake the heavens and the earth. Show Him you're fearless.

God, thank You for the freedom to dream big and ask bigger. I will no longer shy away from requests that feel too much. I will ask away and trust You to answer in whatever way You see fit. In Jesus' name I pray. Amen.

GOOD DECISIONS

When the Lord is pleased with the decisions you've made,
he activates grace to turn enemies into friends.
PROVERBS 16:7 TPT

Don't be afraid to stand alone in making right decisions. It may be an unpopular stand to take, but you'll reap rewards otherwise unattainable. When you make decisions with His will in mind, good things will result. It can be scary to break from the crowd and choose a different path. It may cost you relationships along the way. You may be ridiculed or criticized by those you thought you could count on for support. But God will be pleased because you pushed past your anxiety and followed Him anyway.

Have you made bad choices lately? Have you stayed silent rather than speak up for what's right? Did you compromise your witness because you chose to follow your fleshly desires over God's? Take some time today to talk to the Lord about it. Confess the bad decisions. Discuss your convictions with Him. And ask Him to embolden you so you can make better, godlier decisions in the future. Know that when you do, He will smile and call you courageous.

God, I need wisdom and discernment so I can make
decisions that glorify You. I confess the times I've taken
the easy path of less resistance. Those days are over.
Make me bold as a lion so I have the courage to choose
Your way every time. In Jesus' name I pray. Amen.

YOU CAN'T DERAIL
GOD'S PLAN

With his breath he scatters the schemes of nations who oppose him; they will never succeed. His destiny-plan for the earth stands sure. His forever-plan remains in place and will never fail.

PSALM 33:10–11 TPT

The will of God *will* be done. Make no mistake. And rest assured there is nothing you can do to stop it. Sometimes we worry that our wrong choice messed everything up. We think a bad decision derailed His plans. We carry guilt over a divorce or shame over a moral failure, certain we have ruined it all. We're full of anxiety about quitting a ministry job or volunteer position. We worry that because we didn't finish writing the book we felt commissioned to write, we foiled the plan. Simply not true.

As today's passage reveals, God's plan stands sure and will remain in place without fail. What a relief to realize we don't have to live in fear of changing His plan. We're simply not capable of it. And that frees us up to take bold steps in faith as we follow the Lord. So go ahead and make decisions with confidence without worrying about making mistakes. God will see your faith and call you courageous.

God, what a relief to know I'm not powerful enough to mess up Your plans. I'm grateful You are almighty and all-knowing! In Jesus' name I pray. Amen.

WHEN YOU FEAR BEING UNSEEN

*The Eternal peers down from heaven and watches
all of humanity; He observes every soul from His
divine residence. He has formed every human heart,
breathing life into every human spirit; He knows
the deeds of each person, inside and out.*
PSALM 33:13–15 VOICE

Sometimes one of our greatest fears is not being seen by others. We feel invisible–unnoticed. No one seems to recognize how much our heart is hurting or how vulnerable we're feeling. Maybe this invisibility is in a friendship where our friend seems less interested in our struggles and more focused on theirs. Maybe it's in our marriage, with our husband always busy with work or other projects. Maybe it's as a single mom trying to pay bills with three different jobs and no time for meaningful connection with others. Or maybe it's in our job, where we've been overlooked yet again for a promotion we are well qualified for.

Lay down the fear of not being seen and pick up the truth that God sees you inside and out. He knows your pain. He hears your words of despair. He sees every tear that falls. Take heart, knowing the Lord recognizes the effort it takes to continue on when you feel unappreciated, and rest assured that He calls you courageous.

*God, thank You for seeing me–all of me. Let me
remember Your watchful care when I feel unseen
and unloved. In Jesus' name I pray. Amen.*

THE COURAGE TO CHOOSE GOD

Watch this: God's eye is on those who respect him, the ones who are looking for his love. He's ready to come to their rescue in bad times; in lean times he keeps body and soul together.
PSALM 33:18–19 MSG

Based on today's verse, consider the benefits of pressing into your faith in God when times are hard. Too often we run to others for support. We look to people for wisdom and strategy for the situation we're stuck in. We put our trust in worldly offerings to fix the weighty issues we're facing. When we're scared, we reach for the wrong comforts to soothe our anxiety. And when we choose these things over God, we are quickly reminded of their short-term efficacy.

Let God be the One to calm every worry and concern. Let Him be the reason for your confidence as you navigate life's choppy waters. When you cry out to the Lord for help, scripture says He is ready to rescue. It says He will help you hold it all together. In other words, you're not alone and hopeless. Even more, the burden of fixing the situation doesn't have to rest on your shoulders. Choose God and know He calls that choice courageous.

God, remind me to look to You when I need help.
This world offers no good solutions for my heart;
You alone do. In Jesus' name I pray. Amen.

WITH ALL HE'S GOT

*We're depending on G*OD*; he's everything we need.*
What's more, our hearts brim with joy since we've
*taken for our own his holy name. Love us, G*OD*, with*
all you've got—that's what we're depending on.

PSALM 33:20–22 MSG

God loves you with all He is. He holds nothing back when it comes to His generous love for His children. It's a gift that is lavishly poured out for us without expectation, so be careful not to let any insecurity or worry change that narrative in your mind. God's devotion isn't something you have to earn or work to keep. It doesn't increase or decrease based on your works. Even more, no amount of sinning will cancel it out. And even when you're angry with the Lord or walk away for a season, His love never changes.

Be honest. Are you scared of losing God's affection for one reason or another? When you mess up, do you worry your actions will somehow change His love for you? Let today's verse reaffirm that His love is unshakable. You can depend on it. And, friend, it's because of His love that He will be everything you need to navigate this life well. Be courageous in believing this truth, and let God see your faith in action!

God, I trust You to love me with all You have,
and I believe in my heart Your love for me will
never change! In Jesus' name I pray. Amen.

YOUR EVERYTHING

*GOD, my shepherd! I don't need a thing. You have
bedded me down in lush meadows, you find me quiet
pools to drink from. True to your word, you let me
catch my breath and send me in the right direction.*

PSALM 23:1–3 MSG

Maybe your heart is weary right now and the words of today's scripture passage sound too good to be true. Maybe things in your world are confusing and exhausting, and you're barely holding on. Like others, maybe you've been going ninety miles an hour for so long that you're afraid if you slow down you will crater. And maybe you don't know who to turn to or what you really need as you seek peace. Friend, is this you today?

Don't shy away from asking the Lord to be your everything. Be bold as you ask Him to meet every need facing you right now. Ask God to examine your heart and mind and to help you understand the roots of your fears and insecurities. Ask Him to bring peace into those chaotic places inside that keep you awake at night. Ask Him to calm the anxious thoughts that stir your emotions. And then surrender to His leading, trusting the Shepherd to meet every need. God calls this way of living courageous.

*God, please be my everything until I realize I have
all I need in You. In Jesus' name I pray. Amen.*

YOUR ENEMIES WILL WATCH

You prepare a banquet for me, where all my enemies
can see me; you welcome me as an honored
guest and fill my cup to the brim. I know that your
goodness and love will be with me all my life; and
your house will be my home as long as I live.
PSALM 23:5–6 GNT

Sometimes the idea of getting revenge seems sweet, doesn't it? When others hurt us, getting back at them feels justified and so we spend ridiculous amounts of time strategizing. We think about what we'd say to them if we had the chance. We formulate plans to expose the injustice to others, hoping to embarrass them. We find ways to work their trespasses into conversations with friends and family as we try to ruin their reputation. But God already has a plan.

Imagine attending a beautiful banquet as the honored guest. God is the host who has prepared an elaborate meal and table. It's immaculate in every way. And off to the side are your enemies–those who have hurt you. Their jaws have dropped at the powerful moment they are witnessing. Right then and there, they realize your immeasurable value to the King. Friend, have the courage to let God be the One to deal with your enemies.

God, thank You for promising to handle my enemies so
I don't risk sinning by plotting revenge. Instead, I will
rest in Your goodness. In Jesus' name I pray. Amen.

EVERY TEAR IS NOTICED

*For when the cords of death wrapped around me
and torrents of destruction overwhelmed me, taking
me to death's door, in my distress I cried out to you, the
delivering God, and from your temple-throne you heard
my troubled cry, and my sobs went right into your heart.*
PSALM 18:4–6 TPT

Every tear you cry is noticed by the Lord. Isn't that a beautiful promise? Sometimes we're afraid He is too busy to notice our broken heart. We think He doesn't have time to hear our cry or to help us with the little things. We think God has bigger fish to fry, so we try to handle our worries on our own. And even when our struggle feels gigantic to us, we realize we're but one person in a world full of people. We decide that since the Lord is busy with countries and famine and poverty, our tears are more of a burden than a concern.

Rest assured—backed by scripture—God notices you. He sees every burden you carry and every fear that comes with them. That means every sob that escapes is heard, and every tear that falls is seen. And even more, His purpose is to rescue you. Don't stop crying out to the Lord. He will honor the courage it takes to do so.

*God, see my troubled cry and rescue me!
In Jesus' name I pray. Amen.*

PULLED FROM ENEMY HATE

But me he caught—reached all the way from sky to sea;
he pulled me out of that ocean of hate, that enemy chaos,
the void in which I was drowning. They hit me when I
was down, but GOD stuck by me. He stood me up on a
wideopen field; I stood there saved—surprised to be loved!

PSALM 18:16–18 MSG

Can you relate to the psalmist's words about being in an ocean of hate? Have you ever felt like you were caught in enemy chaos? Have you ever been under the weight of so much fear that you felt as if you were drowning? Maybe you understand the psalmist's feeling of being hit while already down with the hurtful punches coming one after another. There seems to be no shortage of tough and scary situations we have to endure. But it's vital we remember we're not alone.

Maybe you didn't realize it in the moment, but every time you have cried out to the Lord, He has caught you. He is not a faraway God who keeps His distance. No. He is an ever-present God who reaches down from heaven to save you. He pulls you from the void of worry and anxiety and gives you breathing room. So don't ever sit in your fear alone. Be quick to ask God to rescue you. Your courage won't go unnoticed.

God, pull me from enemy hate. I need
Your help! In Jesus' name I pray. Amen.

FOCUSED ON HIS
RIGHTEOUS WORDS

*He rewarded me for doing what's right and staying pure.
I will follow his commands and I'll not sin by ceasing to
follow him, no matter what. For I've kept my eyes focused
on his righteous words, and I've obeyed everything
that he's told me to do. I've been blameless before him
and followed all his ways, keeping my heart pure.*

PSALM 18:20–23 TPT

One of the smartest things we can do as we navigate tough situations is keep our eyes focused on the righteous words of God. He wrote them as a way of revealing Himself to those who love Him. They are meant to challenge and encourage your heart. They are designed to bring perspective and strategy to mind. And the Bible is loaded with wisdom that will calm your nerves. It's a powerful weapon in your arsenal.

When you focus on the fresh revelation in its pages rather than concentrating on what causes anxiety, you will come out the other side victorious. You'll find sure footing and the ability to stand strong through every season of struggle. Moreover, taking His Word to heart and following His direction will open the door for God to recognize and bless your courageous obedience.

*God, thank You for Your Word and the way it brings
confidence to my heart. In Jesus' name I pray. Amen.*

LET GOD BE
YOUR FLOODLIGHT

God, all at once you turned on a floodlight for me!
You are the revelation-light in my darkness, and in
your brightness I can see the path ahead. . . . What
a perfect God you are! All Yahweh's promises have
proven true. What a secure shelter for all those who
turn to hide themselves in you, the wraparound God.

PSALM 18:28, 30 TPT

Have you ever lost power in your home in the middle of the night? In the pitch black that surrounds you, fear creeps in as you try to find a flashlight to illuminate the room. When that ray of light breaks through the darkness, you instantly feel calmer. Your eyes can focus on familiar things. Your anxiousness subsides. And you feel stronger and braver.

Regardless of what you're going through—relationship struggles, parenting woes, financial stress, or deep insecurities—let God be the floodlight in your heart. Let Him shine the light of His love into each situation and bring peace. Let His glow melt every fear away. When you ask Him, the Lord will show you the path out of darkness and into His brightness. Clinging to God will show your courage, and He will call it out.

God, I'm surrounded by so much darkness and desperate
for You to shine Your brightness into every situation and
illuminate Your path for my life. In Jesus' name I pray. Amen.

GOD'S WRAPAROUND PRESENCE

*You empower me for victory with your wraparound
presence. Your power within makes me strong
to subdue. By stooping down in gentleness, you
made me great! You've set me free, and now I'm
standing complete, ready to fight some more!*
PSALM 18:35–36 TPT

Did you know that God has a wraparound presence? Even more, do you know what that means for you? Consider the amazingness of this statement and let it sink in. This wraparound presence means the Lord has you covered on every side. There's no part of you, friend, that's exposed. Can you visualize it? His love and protection are all-encompassing. Being surrounded by them gives you strength to handle anything life throws in your path. It gives you confidence. It brings freedom. And remember, you can't be in bondage from slavery and empowered for victory at the same time.

How does this truth make a difference in your heart today? How does it grow your faith and trust in God? Take time to thank Him for loving you enough to wrap His holy presence around your life. Tell Him how that knowledge changes things for you. Ask for this gift to be at the forefront of your mind the next time fear and worry creep in. And remember that because of His great love for you, you can deal courageously with whatever comes your way.

*God, You are amazing. Thank You for wrapping
me in Your love. In Jesus' name I pray. Amen.*

HE WILL EQUIP YOU FOR BATTLE

*For You equipped me for battle, and You made
my enemies fall beneath me. You made my
enemies turn tail and run, and all who wanted my
destruction, I destroyed. They looked everywhere,
but no one came to rescue them; they asked
the Eternal, but He did not answer them.*

PSALM 18:39–41 VOICE

No matter what battles you are facing at this very moment, God will equip you for them. That isn't a hope or something to work toward. No. This is the reality of having a relationship with the Lord.

So often we feel ill-equipped to deal with what comes our way. We give in to fear, allowing it to paralyze us. We're scared of saying the wrong things. We're worried our actions may be misinterpreted. Our insecurities get the best of us and we cower in feelings of *I'm not good enough*. And in the end, we are ineffective. But, friend, the Lord is ready and able to equip you to stand strong in every battle. You are strong because of His power. You are wise because of His discernment. Don't waste any time on worry, scared you can't handle the situation. Call on God to equip you, and He will call you His courageous one.

*God, I trust You to give me every weapon necessary to
be victorious in the battles I face! Thank You for Your
promise to equip me. In Jesus' name I pray. Amen.*

HIS POWER REVEALED IN YOU

*"But I have kept you in power for a reason, to show
you My greater power and to see that My name
and reputation spread through all the earth."*
EXODUS 9:16 VOICE

Can you think of someone who navigated a rough season of life with unexpected grace? You were waiting for them to crumble, but they didn't. You expected them to give up or give in, but they stood strong instead. They smiled when most would be in tears, and they loved when others would be an angry mess. When the punches kept coming, you watched in awe as they continued taking the next step day after day. And when you asked how they did it, they gave all the glory to God.

Consider the truth that God shows His power through His people. It not only benefits us but blesses others too! Think of a time when you saw this principle play out in your own life. Maybe you managed a tough season with your teenager or navigated the sudden loss of a parent. And rather than throw in the towel, you allowed God to strengthen you. Against all odds, you had courage for the next day. The truth is that God uses your life to reveal His power. Your bravery is beautiful, and your *yes* gets His attention.

*God, use me to reflect Your strength and
power! In Jesus' name I pray. Amen.*

HE WILL STICK WITH YOU

"Yes. I'll stay with you, I'll protect you wherever you go, and I'll bring you back to this very ground. I'll stick with you until I've done everything I promised you."
GENESIS 28:15 MSG

Don't worry, friend. If God has called you to something, you can be sure He will be right there with you every step of the way. Others may flake out or get bored with the process, but the Lord never tires. He is patient and kind and knows the perfect timing of all things. You are in good hands.

So what is God doing in your life right now? Where is He leading you? What has He asked of you? Rest assured that God fully understands what you need to complete the task. He sees every pitfall that may disrupt your journey. He knows the fears and insecurities whispering in your ear. He is aware of what may try to pull your attention away from Him. That is exactly why God promises to protect you and finish the work He started in you. Your job? Have courageous faith to follow the Lord's leading. He is well pleased with your willing heart, and your bravery delights Him!

God, please stay close to me. Guide me as I place my trust in You. Open my eyes to see the path You have for me, and make me courageous as I travel it with You. In Jesus' name I pray. Amen.

THE COURAGE TO HELP

This is how we have discovered love's reality:
Jesus sacrificed his life for us. Because of this great love,
we should be willing to lay down our lives for one another.
If anyone sees a fellow believer in need and has the means
to help him, yet shows no pity and closes his heart against
him, how is it even possible that God's love lives in him?

1 JOHN 3:16–17 TPT

How often do we see others in need and find justification for not intervening? Think about it. You may pass someone asking for money on the side of the road. You may see images of natural disasters in places other than your own community. A family at your child's school may have suffered a sudden tragedy. A couple at church may be getting a divorce. But in our fear, we do nothing.

We may worry we'll say the wrong thing and offend someone, or they'll reject our help and hurt our feelings. Their situation may hit too close to our own, picking the scab off a wound we've been trying to heal. We may feel completely inadequate to help in any way. But God is asking for you to reach out in compassion. Even if it feels uncomfortable, you're extending the Lord's hands to others. Ask Him for confidence. And know when you take that step of faith toward another, He will call you courageous.

God, help me love others well. In Jesus' name I pray. Amen.

HOW TO LIVE IN BOLD FREEDOM

Whenever our hearts make us feel guilty and remind us of our failures, we know that God is much greater and more merciful than our conscience, and he knows everything there is to know about us. My delightfully loved friends, when our hearts don't condemn us, we have a bold freedom to speak face-to-face with God.

1 JOHN 3:20–21 TPT

Guilt and shame are a big deal because their end goal is condemnation. And while many think they're one and the same, they are not. Guilt says you've done something bad, but shame says you are bad. And they both remind you of times you've failed in the past, keeping you fearful of trying again. But, friend, you don't have to live this way another day.

God wants you to be free. He knows the weight of guilt and shame affects every part of your life, especially your relationship with Him. And rather than take this burden directly to the Lord, you're likely tempted to try to hide from Him. So today, right now, share it all with God. He sees every part of you—the good and the not so good—and loves you completely. If you want to live in the bold freedom He promises, then have the courage to ask for it. He'll see your brave move and honor it.

God, remove my shame and guilt so I can live confidently in the freedom You promise. In Jesus' name I pray. Amen.

COURAGE TO TRUST AND LOVE

So these are his commands: that we continually place our trust in the name of his Son, Jesus Christ, and that we keep loving one another, just as he has commanded us. For all who obey his commands find their lives joined in union with him, and he lives and flourishes in them. We know and have proof that he constantly lives and flourishes in us, by the Spirit that he has given us.

1 JOHN 3:23–24 TPT

Sometimes it takes all we have to follow God because what He asks is humanly impossible. It really does take everything we've got plus His help to obey the commands put before us. But it's important we remember He isn't a dictator and we His subjects. Instead, God's commands are designed to help us live the best life possible, and obedience always brings a blessing. Never forget this powerful truth.

When the Lord tells us to trust Him and love others, we might hesitate because we know these are tall orders requiring bold faith and courageous compassion. But when we ask for His help to live with both, scripture says our life will flourish with God's goodness. He will give us the ability to walk out His will. And the Lord will call brave those who live with gusto.

God, give me the courage to trust You and love others. I need Your help to live this way. In Jesus' name I pray. Amen.

BE A BOLD TRUTH-TELLER

Delightfully loved friends, don't trust every spirit, but carefully
examine what they say to determine if they are of God,
because many false prophets have mingled into the world.
Here's the test for those with the genuine Spirit of God: they
will confess Jesus as the Christ who has come in the flesh.

1 JOHN 4:1–2 TPT

- -

Don't be afraid to ask questions of someone who is proclaiming God's name. There's nothing wrong with examining their words against what the Bible says. Trust the Holy Spirit in you and take notice when something sits wrong in your gut. You have access to His divine discernment, so don't be scared to disagree. You have His permission to be bold in your doubt.

Remember that you're a force to be reckoned with, friend. Because you follow God, you're a truth-teller here on earth. Your commission is to be a light in this dark world, and you do that by standing in your God-given authority. Don't allow fear of man to keep you from speaking out. Don't let insecurity stop you from standing up for truth. Ask the Lord to build your confidence in Him so your life will shine His light. Your steadfastness won't escape His notice, and He will call you His courageous warrior.

God, help me know when something is not right, and give
me courage to question it. In Jesus' name I pray. Amen.

BE CONFIDENT GOD HEARS YOU

*We live in the bold confidence that God hears our
voices when we ask for things that fit His plan. And if
we have no doubt that He hears our voices, we can
be assured that He moves in response to our call.*

1 JOHN 5:14–15 VOICE

Make no mistake—God hears you! He hears your every request for His help, every plea for His rescue. When you need wisdom and discernment in certain situations, the Lord hears you ask for them. He listens to every guttural response to your broken heart and responds to your pleas for fearlessness. You can have bold confidence that every petition you place before God that fits into His plan for your life is fully heard and understood by Him.

Even more, once that truth sinks deep into the marrow of your bones, you can be 100 percent assured that He will answer you. So today, tell the Lord what you need in your life. Let Him know your heart's desires. Share your fears and concerns, asking for His divine intervention. Be brave as you open up before your Father in heaven, knowing you're heard. Show Him your courageous faith.

*God, what a privilege to know You hear me when I
pray. Would You give me the courage to be bold in
my requests and the discernment to ask according to
Your plan for my life? In Jesus' name I pray. Amen.*

HE WILL GRIP YOUR HAND

*"I am Yahweh, your mighty God! I grip your
right hand and won't let you go! I whisper to
you: 'Don't be afraid; I am here to help you!' "*
ISAIAH 41:13 TPT

Sometimes—especially when we're scared—we just want someone to hold our hand. We feel desperate for a hug because we need reassurance that everything will be okay. We want someone to walk through the difficult times with us so we don't feel all alone. The truth is that it can be incredibly comforting to have a companion to encourage and support us. But too often we don't have anyone who will. And the fear inside us grows as we realize we must navigate things on our own.

Friend, you are never alone. Scripture says that God will grip your hand and not let go. Even if every friend or family member walks away in your time of need, the Lord never will. He is there through every up and down. You don't have to be scared because He's right there, whispering reminders to have courage and to trust that He is with you. Imagine, the One who created the heavens and earth never leaves your side. Take heart and be strong, because you're backed by the Almighty. Grab His hand and show Him your courageous spirit!

*God, thank You for Your promise to hold my hand in scary times.
I'm so grateful for Your presence. In Jesus' name I pray. Amen.*

LAWLESS VS. LOVER

*The lawless are haunted by their fears and what they
dread will come upon them, but the longings of the
lovers of God will all be fulfilled. The wicked are blown
away by every stormy wind. But when a catastrophe
comes, the lovers of God have a secure anchor.*

PROVERBS 10:24–25 TPT

Today's verses include a powerful contrast that is worthy of recognition. Did you notice the different outcomes experienced by the lawless and wicked versus the lovers of God? Sometimes it seems those who do bad things always win out, but that's not true. The reality is they are forever haunted by their fears. They worry about the future. And when the storms of life rise up, they are tossed about relentlessly. They have nothing of substance to keep them grounded.

But notice what happens to those who love God. They will be fulfilled in life. Their hearts' desires will come to pass. And when tough seasons come their way, their faith anchors them. Fear doesn't win out. Insecurities don't strangle their heart. Choose today to be a lover of God and to live your life for Him. Let Him be the reason you are confident and secure. When you choose this path, God will bless your courageous decision to love Him.

*God, I love You and I will choose You
every day. In Jesus' name I pray. Amen.*

THE CONFIDENCE TO SPEAK OUT

*Speak out on behalf of those who have no voice,
and defend all those who have been passed
over. Open your mouth, judge fairly, and stand
up for the rights of the afflicted and the poor.*
PROVERBS 31:8-9 VOICE

Speaking out for what's right can be scary because it opens us up to being judged. With the proverbial spotlight shining our direction, we might feel intimidated about speaking up for justice. But consider that's exactly why God has you in this moment. It might be your turn to say what needs to be said, waking people up. Your voice might be the best one to proclaim the truth.

It's okay to feel scared. Your nerves don't have to be calm before you open your mouth to speak. You don't have to feel a deep sense of peace before you defend the rights of others. Anything worth doing takes guts and grit. So ask God for bravery, friend. Ask for the confidence necessary to walk out His will. And know when you say yes to God's call on your life, He will recognize your courage and delight in it.

*God, I want to do as You please, but I need a big
dose of courage. I'm afraid of opening myself up to
criticism. I'm scared of being judged. But even more
than that, I want to follow You. I trust that You will
give me all I need. In Jesus' name I pray. Amen.*

TALK IT OUT WITH GOD FIRST

I love the LORD, because he hears me; he listens to my prayers. He listens to me every time I call to him. The danger of death was all around me; the horrors of the grave closed in on me; I was filled with fear and anxiety. Then I called to the LORD, "I beg you, LORD, save me!"

PSALM 116:1–4 GNT

When we're in a tough situation, we just need to talk it out. We need to chew on the details and ruminate on the way things have played out so far. We need to unpack our feelings and fears as we try to wrap our mind around the events of the day. Silence may be needed for a short time, but eventually we'll need to process until we've exhausted every last thought. Amen?

But what about the times no one is around? What about when we've exhausted those around us? What if they don't want to talk it over again? Their indifference can hurt our feelings, trigger insecurities, and discourage us. It's important to keep in mind that God is always ready and willing to listen. He hears your prayers and your cries for help. And He will listen to every fear and anxious thought. Friend, talk things out with God first. That bold move will please His heart!

God, I will come to You first to talk things out. Thank You for always wanting to hear what I have to say! In Jesus' name I pray. Amen.

THE POWER OF SELF-TALK

The LORD is merciful and good; our God is
compassionate. The LORD protects the helpless;
when I was in danger, he saved me. Be confident,
my heart, because the LORD has been good to me.
PSALM 116:5-7 GNT

Do you talk to yourself? Chances are you do—we all do. But most of us say horrible things rather than voice positive reinforcements. We're critical because we forgot to buy eggs at the grocery store. We tell ourselves we're stupid for the comment we just made at the office. We ridicule the meal we made or the way we wrapped a gift. More than anyone else, we're often our own worst enemy. Is that you?

The psalmist gives us a beautiful example of positive self-talk when we're feeling uncertain. In those moments when you're afraid or unsure, why not remind yourself of all God has done for you? Why not speak out about the times He came through or the ways He equipped you for the battle? Be kind to yourself, friend. You are the daughter of the King! So be bold with your declarations and always speak encouraging words of power and truth. Doing so will help you live in victory, and God will delight in His confident daughter!

God, I confess I am unkind with the words I say to
myself. Help me be more mindful to say generous and
compassionate things instead. In Jesus' name I pray. Amen.

KEEP ON BELIEVING

*The LORD saved me from death; he stopped my tears
and kept me from defeat. And so I walk in the presence
of the LORD in the world of the living. I kept on believing,
even when I said, "I am completely crushed," even
when I was afraid and said, "No one can be trusted."*
PSALM 116:8–11 GNT

The reality is that sometimes we must fake it till we make it. Think about it. Have you ever struggled to grab onto your faith? It's not that you didn't believe in the Lord, but your situation felt heavy and over-whelming. You momentarily doubted He would come through for you this time, even though He has so many times before. You believed, but you needed help with your unbelief. Take heart. Faith requires great courage when things around you seem to be falling apart. And in some circumstances we must find the courage to believe based solely on our past experiences with God.

In those moments, focus your mind on every time He has saved you. Think of the times you saw His hand move mightily in a situation you thought was too big. Those are the moments that refresh your belief and enable you to take the next step. And when you do, God will call your faith fearless.

*God, help my faith stay strong even when I battle unbelief.
I know You are my God! In Jesus' name I pray. Amen.*

GIVING GOD EVERY PRAISE

I will offer all my loving praise to you, and I thank you so much for answering my prayer and bringing me salvation!
PSALM 118:21 TPT

Don't forget to give God praise for all He has done for you. Has He delivered you from paralyzing fear? Untangled you from the web of your insecurities? Restored your heart for a husband who betrayed you? Allowed you to find forgiveness you never thought possible? Healed a heart broken from grief? Opened the door to a new job? Brought unexpected financial relief? Miraculously removed a disease? The Lord is in the business of answering prayers in beautiful ways, and we need to give Him the glory.

Why not spend time in prayer right now, thanking Him for all the ways He has moved in your life. Maybe get down on your knees or lie prostrate before Him. Maybe create your own song of praise or dance your heart out. Don't be afraid to try something new as you show Him your gratitude. Your bold stance of appreciation won't go unnoticed—He will delight in the way you share your thankful heart with Him.

God, forgive me for the times I've forgotten to thank You. I never want to make You feel unappreciated. I know You are the reason for the good things in my life. Thank You! In Jesus' name I pray. Amen.

WHEN YOU'RE
FEELING INADEQUATE

*I stood before you feeling inadequate, filled
with reverence for God, and trembling under
the sense of the importance of my words.*
1 CORINTHIANS 2:3 TPT

We all feel the fear of inadequacy from time to time. There are things we must do that seem terrifying, and we just don't feel up for the job. Sometimes we focus on all the times we tried and failed. We feel too old for the task or too young to be taken seriously. We worry someone will see right through the facade and ridicule us. And while there certainly may be people who think we're not good enough, their opinion doesn't negate what God thinks.

Stand tall, mighty one. The Lord will fully equip you to walk out the calling on your life. He will help you overcome the fear of failure by firming up your level of confidence. God will give you wisdom and discernment to know what is best. It's normal to battle anxiety because you want to do a good job. The jitters and flutters are common reactions to stepping out of your comfort zone. But when you ask the Lord to fill in the gaps where you lack courage, He will. And your willingness to put yourself out there will show Him your bold faith.

*God, I'm trusting You to help me overcome those yucky
feelings of inadequacy. In Jesus' name I pray. Amen.*

DELIVERANCE FROM EVIL

*And my Lord will continue to deliver me from every form
of evil and give me life in his heavenly kingdom. May all
the glory go to him alone for all the ages of eternity!*

2 TIMOTHY 4:18 TPT

Evil comes in many forms and is called by many different names. Immorality. Sinfulness. Maliciousness. Corruption. Wickedness. Evil is what causes difficult, painful seasons in marriage. It's what makes people say things to hurt others. It clouds our ability to make good choices and keeps us from doing what we know is right. Evil brings terrible events into our lives, draining our joy. It fuels mean-spiritedness and causes people to turn against one another. It robs us of security and peace. And it breeds deep insecurity and fear.

Friend, no matter what you're battling at this moment, trust God with it. Believe He sees everything and is working on your behalf right now. His beautiful promise to rescue isn't only for a few elite people. It isn't saved for the most holy. God is in the deliverance business and His eyes are always on you. This season will pass, and you will be saved. Stand tall today and know that when you choose to trust Him over everything else, God will call you courageous.

*God, I feel the evil around me these days and I'm asking
for deliverance. I know You're working things out, and
I will wait patiently. In Jesus' name I pray. Amen.*

COURAGE TO ACCEPT
THE CALL OF LEADERSHIP

*When you shepherd the flock God has given you, watch
over them not because you have to but because you
want to. For this is how God would want it not because
you're being compensated somehow but because you
are eager to watch over them. Don't lead them as if
you were a dictator, but lead your flock by example.*

1 PETER 5:2–3 VOICE

Being a leader is a privilege, not a burden. Speaking truth into the lives
of others is an honor. So when God calls you up, take it seriously. Out
of your own fear and insecurity, you may think leadership is a mistake.
You may wonder if God has lost His marbles. But trust that He knows
exactly what He's doing: There is something inside you that He wants
to cultivate. You were chosen on purpose.

Have faith in moments like these, taking on the mantle the Lord
created you to wear. Don't allow anxiety to steal it. Be prayerful and
purposeful to lead God's way. Show others how to live by your example. And guard your heart against anything that might cheapen this
opportunity or cause you to feel resentment. God sees something
amazing in you, friend, so stand tall and say yes. Let the Lord see His
brave daughter step forward in trust and faith.

*God, I'll follow Your plan for my life.
In Jesus' name I pray. Amen.*

CHOOSING JOY

My fellow believers, when it seems as though you are facing nothing but difficulties, see it as an invaluable opportunity to experience the greatest joy that you can! For you know that when your faith is tested it stirs up in you the power of endurance. And then as your endurance grows even stronger, it will release perfection into every part of your being until there is nothing missing and nothing lacking.

JAMES 1:2–4 TPT

Are you facing nothing but difficulties right now? Is life throwing the worst it has to offer at you? No doubt these seasons are terrible on many fronts because they take a toll in every way. But what if you changed your perspective? It's a bold move, but what if you chose to see these times as invaluable opportunities to grow your faith? That deliberate shift in focus has the ability to bring joy.

These scary and frustrating times test our faith. But God uses them to our benefit and His glory. They birth in us endurance to stand strong, unwilling to let fear take us out. And with that endurance, we become bold and brave. The joy comes as we allow this newfound confidence to replace discouragement, and it is beautiful to behold! Friend, your willingness to choose joy no matter what won't go unnoticed by God— He will be delighted to see it.

God, I choose joy! In Jesus' name I pray. Amen.

BE BOLD IN YOUR ASK FOR WISDOM

But if any of you lack wisdom, you should pray to God, who will give it to you; because God gives generously and graciously to all. But when you pray, you must believe and not doubt at all. Whoever doubts is like a wave in the sea that is driven and blown about by the wind.

JAMES 1:5–6 GNT

Don't be afraid to ask God for wisdom. This life is impossible without it; we need solid guidance to live well. Sometimes we struggle to know the best health choices. Sometimes we're not sure about the best use of money. Often we fumble in our relationships because we don't know the best move to make. And how do we parent with purpose when we lack a full understanding of the issues at hand? Rest assured God knows it all.

So pray! Ask the Lord to give you wisdom as often as you need it. Confess your fears and insecurities about making decisions and listen for His guidance. And pray with full confidence that God will show you what's next because it matters. Doubt will derail you. Be bold and courageous in your requests and watch how God responds!

God, I need Your help to know what's next and what's best. I know You will guide me! In Jesus' name I pray. Amen.

DON'T GIVE UP

*Anyone who meets a testing challenge head-on and
manages to stick it out is mighty fortunate. For such persons
loyally in love with God, the reward is life and more life.*

JAMES 1:12 MSG

Stand strong, warrior! Your situation may look bleak, but God is working. Your child may be fighting you at every turn, but the Lord is with you as you love and parent. Your financial situation may have taken a turn for the worse, but He sees your needs. You husband may have broken your heart, but the Lord is right by your side. Don't give in to the whispers to give up. With God, you are not weak! His desire is for you to rise up in faith and believe He is at work.

Here is a powerful truth to cling to in these difficult seasons: Your steadfastness will be rewarded. The Lord watches as your weary heart continues to move forward. He sees every time you get back up. And He knows you're choosing to trust Him above all else. He is well aware of your loyalty and will bless you abundantly for it. So let Him see your courage, mighty one. He will honor your perseverance!

*God, I will trust in You at all times. Help me
walk this out! In Jesus' name I pray. Amen.*

COURAGE TO OWN
YOUR OWN SIN

Don't let anyone under pressure to give in to evil say, "God is trying to trip me up." God is impervious to evil, and puts evil in no one's way. The temptation to give in to evil comes from us and only us. We have no one to blame but the leering, seducing flare-up of our own lust. Lust gets pregnant, and has a baby: sin! Sin grows up to adulthood, and becomes a real killer.

JAMES 1:13–15 MSG

Be strong enough to take responsibility for your own sin. It's important we learn early on to own our missteps. Too often we're quick to blame others. We point our finger at them and claim their actions made us do it. And then there are the times we try to blame our indiscretions on God. Somehow we get confused, choosing to believe He would actually try to trip us up. That, friend, is absolutely not true. Not at all.

Have the courage to admit your own sin. No one living on planet Earth is without it. And something powerful happens when we decide to confess the times our choices were wrong. Yes, this kind of confession is humbling and vulnerable, but your boldness will get God's attention and delight His heart.

God, I confess I deeply dislike owning my own sin. It's embarrassing, but I am done with blaming others, including You. In Jesus' name I pray. Amen.

PUTTING ANGER
IN THE BACKSEAT

*Post this at all the intersections, dear friends: Lead
with your ears, follow up with your tongue, and let
anger straggle along in the rear. God's righteousness
doesn't grow from human anger. So throw all spoiled
virtue and cancerous evil in the garbage. In simple
humility, let our gardener, God, landscape you with
the Word, making a salvation-garden of your life.*

JAMES 1:19–21 MSG

Human anger stifles our faith because it takes the focus off God and
places it on us. When we allow anger to sneak in, it removes the peace
in our heart. It stirs up our emotions. And we end up replaying the event
or the conversation over and over again. But James offers a brilliant
solution: Keep anger in the backseat.

Part of living a courageous life is choosing to do the hard things. It's
taking the high road when the other road would be easier. It's keeping
the focus off you and on the Lord. And it's being brave and standing firm
in what's right. When anger arises, deal with it right then and there. And
let it go. Be confident enough to let God's Word landscape your life.

*God, I don't want anger to have space in my life. Help me
let it go and move on in peace. In Jesus' name I pray. Amen.*

COURAGE TO WALK IT OUT

*If some fail to do what God requires, it's as if
they forget the word as soon as they hear it. One
minute they look in the mirror, and the next they
forget who they are and what they look like.*
JAMES 1:23-24 VOICE

Choose to be the kind of woman who puts into practice what God says. Be bold in your faith so you can walk out your life with purpose and passion. It takes courage to set aside your own fleshly desires to follow the Lord into unchartered territory. But when you do, you'll be richly blessed for it.

If God asks you to forgive, then waste no time. If He requires you to trust Him blindly, say yes. When His Word tells you to love the unlovable, embrace the command with gusto. If you need to step out of your comfort zone, then lace up your sneakers. Your obedience matters to God. And when He speaks to you—whether through His Word or into your spirit—take it seriously. Do all you can to hear His words and take action. Obedience is a bold move of faith, and one that delights the heart of God.

*God, I am going to listen and obey, right away.
Help me hear Your Word and hold it close to
my heart. In Jesus' name I pray. Amen.*

MONITORING YOUR WORDS

If you put yourself on a pedestal, thinking you have become a role model in all things religious, but you can't control your mouth, then think again. Your mouth exposes your heart, and your religion is useless.

JAMES 1:26 VOICE

Today's verse is a powerful reminder to check ourselves. Many of us try to live a good life worthy of following. We put into practice the things that create a deeper relationship with God. We speak about living a life of faith. As we parent, we're purposeful to talk to our kids about Jesus. We volunteer regularly, donate generously, and are always looking for ways to bless others. But too often we don't closely monitor our words.

If we are going to live a courageous life, it's so important to regulate the things we say. Not just some of the time, but all of the time. Why? Because our words tell on our heart. Do you only speak kindly in certain company, but then complain recklessly in the company of others? Do you gossip? Cuss people out? God is asking you to be careful with your words no matter where or with who. Have the courage to control your mouth, and God will bless that choice.

God, let my words be a reflection of my love for You! Let my faith encompass every part of my life. In Jesus' name I pray. Amen.

COURAGE TO CHANGE PATHS

*Now you've got my feet on the life path, all
radiant from the shining of your face. Ever since
you took my hand, I'm on the right way.*
PSALM 16:11 MSG

Don't be afraid to ask for God's help to change the path you're on. He is the best One to redirect your life. Even more, He keeps short accounts and, because of the blood of Jesus, holds nothing against you. There's no need to be embarrassed. There's no reason to feel shame. You're deeply loved by the Lord. And He is always ready and willing to help those He loves.

Of course, it takes courage to make this kind of decision. Leaving behind the old, comfortable ways isn't easy. But a beautiful life is ahead of you when God is at the center. Talk to Him today and unpack what you're feeling. In your vulnerability, tell Him what you're wanting to leave behind. Ask Him for help as you pursue a godly life. Confess it all and ask for a clean slate from this day forward. And ask Him to make you aware of His love for you. He'll see your heart for change, and in His delight He'll call you His courageous one.

*God, I need Your help to change paths in my life.
I want to leave behind the old and embrace the new.
Please guide me! In Jesus' name I pray. Amen.*

GUTS AND GRIT TO CHOOSE JOY

A joyful, cheerful heart brings healing to both body and soul. But the one whose heart is crushed struggles with sickness and depression.
PROVERBS 17:22 TPT

There will always be good reasons for our heart to be crushed. Fear for the future isn't going away. Relationships and frustration go hand in hand. Parenting will require all we've got. Work often brings epic challenges. Health worries may be a continual concern. And the list goes on. No matter how much we try, we will face struggles and battles until we see Jesus face-to-face. But we have a choice.

No doubt it takes guts and grit to choose joy anyway. It's a deliberate decision to find the silver lining when everything feels out of control. But, friend, when you trust God with all your heart, He will always give you reasons for cheerfulness. Even when the outlook is bleak, you can rest in His peace. Have the courage to find this place with Him. Don't give in to fear and heartache; they will only muddy your perspective. When you make the bold decision to choose joy, God will honor it! And He will call you courageous.

God, help me choose joy no matter what life throws my way. I will anchor my trust in You through all of life's ups and downs. In Jesus' name I pray. Amen.

ACCEPTING THE DAY'S EVENTS

This is the day the Eternal God has made;
let us celebrate and be happy today.
PSALM 118:24 VOICE

Have you ever stopped to think that God actually created this day? It's because of Him that we are awake and breathing air. In His infinite wisdom, the Lord decided this day would come to be and so it is. God has allowed it. That also means He knows all it will entail for you. He is aware of every challenge coming your way. He sees every heartache heading your direction. God knows about the frayed nerves, the hope deferred, and the insecurities to be triggered. And still, friend, this is the day God made.

If you want to live with courageous faith, choose to give Him glory no matter what happens in these twenty-four hours. Have the grit to trust God, believing He has allowed the day's events for your benefit and His glory. Choose to rest in His peace instead of getting caught up in the world's chaos. And have the courage to say, "This is the day God has made, and I will be happy." Your resolve won't escape His notice.

God, help me find peace by trusting that You are in
control. Give me perspective to see the bigger picture.
Thank You for today! In Jesus' name I pray. Amen.

EMBRACING A FRESH START

All you saints! Sing your hearts out to GOD!
Thank him to his face! He gets angry once in a while,
but across a lifetime there is only love. The nights of
crying your eyes out give way to days of laughter.
PSALM 30:4–5 MSG

Every day you have a fresh start. Do you realize what a blessing that is? Yesterday may have been full of fear and anxiety. There may have been situations that broke your heart. You may have messed up royally and caused someone else pain. Bad news may have hit hard and unexpectedly. But when you woke up today, you were able to begin again.

The temptation is to carry the difficulties from yesterday into today. And while we may have to work through issues that are ongoing, ask the Lord to wake you with new energy and perspective to tackle what the day brings. Leave as much of yesterday there as you can. Be bold in your request to God for refreshment. And rise each morning with a heart full of joyful expectation and hope as you prepare to walk through the day courageously. Want God to call you His brave one? This will do it.

God, thank You that each day is new and fresh. Help me
grab hold of that truth and walk it out. I know You will help
me wake refreshed! In Jesus' name I pray. Amen.

Scripture Index

OLD TESTAMENT

NEW TESTAMENT

MORE INSPIRATION FOR YOUR BEAUTIFUL SOUL

GOD CALLS YOU WORTHY
978-1-64352-474-0

GOD CALLS YOU FORGIVEN
978-1-64352-637-9

GOD CALLS YOU BEAUTIFUL
978-1-64352-710-9

GOD CALLS YOU LOVED
978-1-64352-804-5

GOD CALLS YOU CHOSEN
978-1-64352-926-4

These delightful devotionals—created just for you—
will encourage and inspire your soul with
deeply rooted truths from God's Word

Flexible Casebound / $12.99 each